T0196569

Simply Redeemed

TITUS 3:3-5

JESSICA C. JEMMOTT, MA

WESTBOW
PRESS®
A DIVISION OF THOMAS NELSON
& ZONDERVAN

WestBow Press books may be ordered through booksellers or by contacting:

WestBow Press
A Division of Thomas Nelson & Zondervan
1663 Liberty Drive
Bloomington, IN 47403
www.westbowpress.com
1 (866) 928-1240

Cover image by Jessica C. Jemmott & Danielle Burkleo.

ISBN: 978-1-5127-6104-7 (sc)
ISBN: 978-1-5127-6103-0 (e)

Library of Congress Control Number: 2016917289

Print information available on the last page.

WestBow Press rev. date: 11/3/2016

Dedicated to every soul who is presented this gift from God

You are … Forgiven. Chosen. Purchased by love.
Simply Redeemed!

#iamredeemed

Contents

Foreword

I am overjoyed to have the opportunity to write the foreword for *Simply Redeemed*, a devotional that is going to change the lives of all who have a chance to turn its pages. I met David and Jessica Jemmott at our church when they were visiting the Green family (Lee and Kimberly) in December 2014. During their visit I grabbed their new baby, Caleb, strictly by unction from Holy Spirit, and began to pray for the baby and their family. I knew immediately that it was something very special about this family. Over time, Jessica began to share with me about this devotional, *Simply Redeemed*. After taking time to review this book I immediately knew by the Spirit that Jessica would ask me to write the foreword. *Simply Redeemed* will unfold how to understand the access that God has freely given you to Him, through the blood of Jesus that was shed on Calvary.

Simply Redeemed is so appropriate because we all must understand that we are redeemed from the hand of the enemy by faith and faith alone. As I have had an opportunity to review this life-changing devotional, I am reminded of what the Word of God teaches in Psalm 107:2, where it says, "Let the redeemed of the Lord say so, Whom He has redeemed from the hand of the adversary" (AMP). This redemption is "simply" because He loved us beyond the love that we are able to have for ourselves. His redemptive power that He displayed for us is a clear example of His unconditional love for us. He understands, far more than we do, that Satan has a desire to sift us as wheat. According to Luke 22:31–32, "Simon, Simon, behold, Satan has demanded permission to sift you like wheat; but I have prayed for you, that your faith may not fail; and you, when once you have turned again, strengthen your brothers" (NASB). This tells us that He is not only our Redeemer, but He is our Chief Intercessor.

Because He has this kind of unconditional love for us, this should give us every reason to worship Him beyond any situation or circumstance with which we are faced. Jessica has made it very clear that we must get back to the heart of worship, because this is the kind of worship that always will get us to the heart of God. John 4 is very clear that these are the kinds of worshippers for which He is searching; worshippers who will worship Him in spirit and truth. This devotional will help you to understand the importance of maintaining this true focus on worship, regardless of what people say about you or who you were.

As I speak to our church at Hope Everlasting Ministry, I often tell our people that I don't need anyone to remind me about my past because I was there; I was an active participant. Not only was I a participant, but I also was the most diligent participant that anyone could ever be. As these types of individuals show up in our lives, we must meditate on Romans 8:1, which says, "Therefore there is now no condemnation for those who are in Christ Jesus" (NASB). When we allow this verse of scripture to reign in our lives, we will be able to overcome our adversary the devil every time he tries to remind us who we use to be and what we use to do.

I pray that as you embark upon this life-changing devotional, it blesses you in a mighty way. I believe it will give you the boldness through scripture to face your day and the difficulty it might bring. It will give you the boldness to face the hard truths that you and your loved ones might face with one another. It will give you the boldness to know that you have access to the Father that could only be granted to us through the death, burial, and resurrection of Jesus Christ. This devotional will be a tool to let you know that all things are truly possible when you believe and have faith in our Lord and Savior Jesus Christ, our Redeemer.

Derrick D. Jordan, DMin.
Senior Pastor
Hope Everlasting Ministry
Trussville, Alabama

Acknowledgments

Being confident of this very thing, that he who began a good work in you
will complete it until the day of Jesus Christ.—Philippians 1:6 (NKJV)

The *idea*, the *promise,* the *fact* that *you* currently have possession of this book is a
true testament to my obedience in following the instruction from the Lord; and
confidence that He will surely fulfill His promises according to this ministry.

I would like to gratefully acknowledge various individuals who have journeyed
with me through this large leap of faith. To my husband, David: I owe you an
insurmountable debt of gratitude as you have not only stood by me but also
guided me at times. Thank you for your support, your prayers, and your ability to
acknowledge and receive my spiritual gifts and the move of God over our lives.
As I continuously receive direction from the Lord to "move," you are always there
to encourage each directive through prayer, wisdom, and words of affirmation.
To our three children, Jordan Alexander, Caleb Jeremiah, and Blaire Isabella: my
prayer is that as each of you journeys through life's experiences, your dad and I
will not be great examples of Christians but rather examples of what it means to
have an authentic relationship with Christ and the ability to use that authenticity
in the relationships that you make with people who come across your paths.

To Dad (our grandfather), David Jemmott Sr.: thank you for speaking life over
my gifts. How I've wished you were here for me to call and share these moments,
but you have a much better view, for "to be absent from the body, is to be present
with the Lord."

To Pop (my grandfather), Richard L. Stokes: thank you for speaking "greater"
over my life as a child and for allowing me to be your "sidekick" as you not only
ministered to those in the church but to the community as well! You instilled in
me the importance of maintaining scripture in my heart, serving others, and the
value of intentional prayer.

To my mom, Angela: thank you for always encouraging my gifts and using "life experiences and God's blessings" to make the Bible relatable, understandable, and applicable.

To my dad, Big Pop: thank you for your ability to be a tangible example of forgiveness, grace, and unconditional love!

To Mommy and Daddy (Jemmott): thank you for your continuous prayers, encouragement, and acceptance of not only a place in your hearts and lives as your "daughter-in-love" but for also receiving and embracing God in me!

To Dr. Derrick D. Jordan (the Hope Everlasting Ministry, Trussville, Alabama): I am especially grateful for your encouragement, your obedience, and your visions. I am excited to see what the Lord has in store for His purpose!

To the ladies of the Simply Redeemed group: thank you for your diligence, transparency, and authenticity as we grew together. And a special thank-you to the family and ministry of Common Grounds Café (Dale City, Virginia) for graciously hosting our group.

To Mrs. Rita Moore ("if that's really your name") thank you for your encouragement and your words through the publishing process, as you stated to me, "Do not allow the enemy to distract you! This book *will* be published, as it was created to fulfill God's purpose!"

To all of those family, friends, ministries, prayer warriors, spiritual counselors, and visionaries who have spoken *life* into *Simply Redeemed* and dedicated time to pray over this ministry: I thank you!

And to *each of you readers*: you have been chosen, handpicked by the Lord to take this journey into an authentic, transparent, and Spirit-led experience with Him.

Introduction
Letter to the Reader

Thank you for joining this Spirit-led move of God—a strategic plan of His that continues to blossom into something more beautiful than I ever could have ever imagined, and now *you* are a part of that plan for His purpose.

You have been handpicked by the Lord to take part in this movement!

In January 2015, after returning to work from maternity leave (I'd given birth to our second-born, Caleb), the Holy Spirit instructed me to start a women's community Bible study and gave me the vision for it to be held at a local café. Initially, my thought was, *Starbucks is too small and inconvenient* (oh, how we can put our God in a box). I was excited about this move from the Lord and shared the vision with a small number of ladies who formed a prayer group at my job, but of course then came all of my excuses for why it was *not* the right time.

Before I knew it, a year passed, and I allowed "life" to take precedence over the direct instruction from the Lord.

On January 4, 2016 (while seven and a half months pregnant with our baby girl, Blaire), I was awakened by the Holy Spirit at four in the morning to "move with urgency!" My response was, "Okay, Lord, if I am to move with this Bible study at this particular time, I need You to provide three things: the location, the women, and guidance on how to lead this study in Your Word." Within a week I received direct guidance to my requests.

1. The appointed location for the Bible study was a café that I had never visited, but with a clear vision I was directed to request permission to host the small group there. To my surprise, this café was an extension of a local church. I approached the owner, and she was excited to host our group. (Common Grounds Café is located in Dale City, Virginia. Next time you're in the area, stop by, and tell them Jessica sent you!)

2. I had the idea to post an informational flyer on Facebook to invite women to join the group. The Holy Spirit, however, said, "No, I will give you the names of those who are to participate at this time."

3. After going to the bookstore and staring at a shelf of Bible study guides and workbooks, the Lord informed me that this study would be completely Spirit-led, as it would be me, Him, and the Word. Later that evening I found an old CD that had been missing for over a year. I put it in my car's CD player as I drove to the grocery store, and the only song on the entire disc that did not skip was "Simply Redeemed" by Heather Headley. After listening to the lyrics with my eyes full of tears, I responded "Yes, Lord!"

With no time to prepare, and moving with urgency, as directed, I sat in front of my laptop with my Bibles, as the Spirit of the Lord directed me for the daily lessons to be sent out to the group. The rest, as they say, is history. Simply Redeemed became a six-week Bible study/devotional that was written daily for a group of women (including me) to whom the Lord was clearly speaking through His Word and application.

I offer this Bible study and devotional (with the leader guide included) to you as this book, *Simply Redeemed,* so that it can go beyond our small group and into homes, churches, and cafés everywhere.

* * *

This is a call to stand before the Lord in acceptance of self and desired growth, while identifying the need to be transparent and authentic, no longer bound by the desire for perfection or to be like someone else for such a time as this.

The Lord has taken care of even the minor details—everything from the title to the logo to the location, participants, and Word. Therefore, I have no choice but to believe that *each* of you will receive a *rhema word* (a personal revelation or utterance) from God, as well as spiritual growth through this study/devotional and that you are chosen to stand and declare that you are "not perfect but simply redeemed," as this ministry continues to grow.

You are … forgiven. Chosen. Purchased by love. *Simply redeemed!*

And now, I invite you to ask the Lord to cause you to be transparent to self and that He will allow you to experience Him in ways that you never have before. As you engage in the pages that are to come, feel our Father's presence; as you wait to hear His voice, pray the prayers that were written as the Spirit spoke through me.

With love,

"At one time we too were foolish, disobedient, deceived and enslaved by all kinds of passions and pleasures. We lived in malice and envy, being hated and hating one another. But when the kindness and love of God our Savior appeared, He saved us, not because of righteous things we had done, but because of his mercy. He saved us through the washing of rebirth and renewal by the Holy Spirit" (Titus 3:3–5 NIV).

www.simplyredeemedt335.com

Simply Redeemed

Before we move forward, when you see the title and the logo what are your thoughts? What does "simply redeemed" mean to you? (Write your answer)

Welcome to the first week of the *Simply Redeemed* Bible study and devotional. I am elated to see how the Lord has moved already as we begin this study together. I would like to share with you how this ministry started so that you will know that you were handpicked by the Lord to take part (this will be a theme throughout this study). If you have not read the "Introduction/Letter to Reader," please go back and do so.

Definition of "simply redeemed" from *Webster's Dictionary*:

Simply: (1) nothing more than: only/merely; (2) without any question

Redeemed: (1) to make something that is [unpleasant] better or acceptable; (2) to buy back [as in stock or bond]

Without *any* question we have been transformed from something that was unpleasant in God's sight and have been made acceptable unto Him, as we were once enslaved to sin but "bought back" with a price on the cross. (Thank You, Jesus!)

1. Read Titus 3:3–5 (NIV).

"At one time we too were foolish, disobedient, deceived and enslaved by all kinds of passions and pleasures. We lived in malice and envy, being hated and hating one another. But when the kindness and love of God our Savior appeared, He saved us, not because of righteous things we had done, but because of his mercy. He saved us through the washing of rebirth and renewal by the Holy Spirit."

2. Go back and read your definition of "simply redeemed." What are your thoughts now?

* * *

Each one of us is an imperfect woman. (Accept it.) As we move forward in this study there will be an opportunity for you to identify areas where you have *already* seen or experienced transformation; areas where you are *still seeking* and asking the Lord for total transformation; and areas where you *did not realize* transformation was necessary (let's crush our egos). However, as the scripture above identifies, we were *once* "foolish, disobedient, deceived, serving various lusts and pleasures, living in malice and envy, hateful and hating one another … but according to His mercy He saved us, through the washing of regeneration and renewing of the Holy Spirit."

Repeat this statement out loud: "I am not perfect; I am redeemed!"

Going Deeper

What is your current relationship status—single, dating, engaged, married, divorced, widowed?

Wherever you are in life right now relationally, you know what you desire in an intimate relationship.

    1. List your top three to five desires or must-haves that identify your view on a truly personal and intimate relationship.

Now that you've completed your list of characteristics that you most likely desire from your mate, what about what your mate desires from you? Review your answers and circle the responses on which you can improve. (Be honest with yourself.)

In every relationship, we experience several stages as it builds, with a goal of reaching true intimacy. There are various relational stages, however every relationship (passionate or platonic) includes an introduction, exploration, development, commitment, and unanimity.

There are times when we can get comfortable in the developmental stage, which then hinders the relationship from moving forward because of our lack of transparency. When you know that your goal is to reach true intimacy within a relationship, but you or the other individual is holding back from going deeper, then the two of you will never truly know one another—and that hinders the ability to obtain intimacy within a relationship.

2. Close your eyes and meditate on the relationships in your life. Do they lack depth due to remaining on the surface? Do you have a hard time being transparent (open/honest/beyond surface)?

What do you think is hindering your ability to go deeper? Is it a fear of rejection? Could it be fear of facing your own insecurities? Or maybe you are self-absorbed, and it's difficult to identify that it's you who lacks transparency, so you project that onto others.

Take this time for a true self-evaluation of this area in your life, and identify your characteristics in the space provided below.

Review your answers from questions 1 and 2. How does that compare to your relationship with the Lord?

It's time to go deeper.

3. What is your current relationship with the Lord?

4. Reflect on what you wrote. How has your current relationship with God changed from your previous relationship with Him? What is your desire for that relationship, moving forward?

5. How has your relationship status with God affected your relationships and interactions with others?

The Lord desires a deep personal and intimate relationship with you.

6. Read Ephesians 1. (The apostle Paul is writing a letter to the church at Ephesus.) What does the Holy Spirit reveal to you in that chapter?

This scripture reveals that not only are we redeemed but that we ought to also desire an intimate relationship with the Lord and receive a deeper experiential knowledge of Him.

7.   Meditate for a moment on the following passage from Ephesians 1. Let us end in prayer

For this reason, because I have heard of your faith in the Lord Jesus and your love for all God's people, I do not cease to give thanks for you, remembering you in my prayers; [I always pray] that the God of our Lord Jesus Christ, the Father of glory, may grant you a spirit of wisdom and of revelation [that gives you a deep and personal and intimate insight] into the true knowledge of Him [for we know the Father through the Son]. And [I pray] that the eyes of your heart [the very center and core of your being] may be enlightened [flooded with light by the Holy Spirit], so that you will know and cherish the hope [the divine guarantee, the confident expectation] to which He has called you, the riches of His glorious inheritance in the saints (God's people), and [so that you will begin to know] what the immeasurable and unlimited and surpassing greatness of His [active, spiritual] power is in us who believe. These are in accordance with the working of His mighty strength. (Ephesians 1:15–19 AMP)

* * *

Father, I thank You for the completion of day two. Lord, thank You for speaking through Your Word as we are encouraged to obtain a deep, personal, and intimate relationship with You, while identifying the need to move beyond the surface and become increasingly transparent. Father allow us to be humbled as we draw closer to You. While it is our desire to go deeper in our intimate relationship with You, Lord, we ask that You also allow us to see where we fall short in our relationships with others, whether that is our coworkers, friends, family, mate, fiancé, or spouse. Help us, Lord, to continue to become the virtuous women that you desire for us to be, according to Your Word. Amen.

Chosen

You did not choose me but I chose you.—John 15:16

When the Enemy Creeps In

On day one, I shared that you were handpicked by the Lord for this Bible study, but being *chosen* comes with a price. Allow this to be a warning: within this six-week study, if you have not yet experienced a spiritual attack or distraction from the enemy since your commitment to this study, *you will*. Do not let that discourage you, for you are protected. As we move forward in the study, we will go deeper into understanding the battle of the enemy.

> "The enemy does not try to affect things that have value. Because we are chosen, we have value."—Dr. Derrick D. Jordan

It starts with distraction.

Yesterday started out rough but that was to be expected, as I am currently thirty-six weeks pregnant and also have a fifteen-month-old and am home-schooling my four-year old. It was grocery day. After providing breakfast, writing out my grocery list, and getting the boys bathed and dressed, we finally made it out the house. By that time they were ready for lunch, so I made a detour to grab them something to eat (and we had to go back due to a mistake with the order).

When I arrived to the grocery store, I sat in the car for ten minutes to mentally prepare myself for the next three hours. (That's how long it takes, even with a detailed list.)

"Clean up in the meat department." A sippy-cup full of water now no longer full. A trail of chicken nuggets on the floor. Being asked repeatedly, "Mommy, can we get that?" I have never been more relieved to swipe my credit card at the checkout, as it was a clear indicator that it was time to go home—but not before making one more stop at another store for toiletries (bargain shopping.).

When we got through the line at the checkout, I realized that I'd left my wallet in the car. We went back out—and did I mention it was raining? I got my wallet, paid for the groceries, and now finally home.

Allow me to be transparent with you. Normally, I can be easily frustrated, yet throughout the day I remained calm. The only thing on my mind was wanting to get started on the study for day three.

With groceries put away, it was time to start dinner: herb-and-cheese-stuffed flank steak, garlic sautéed asparagus, and honey-glazed carrots.

The kids were in the kitchen, playing and screaming and crying, but it was okay. "Dinner is almost done," I told them. I took the meat out of the oven, which was set to 425 degrees and then at broil for the final fifteen minutes. My husband (David) was on his way out to the gym, and then it happened. Before I knew it, I was screaming and crying and on the floor, holding on to David's waist for dear life. I thought if I let go, my hand might end up on the floor next to me. Without thinking, I'd taken the steel pan out from under the broiler and had grabbed it with my bare hand.

As we made our way to the hospital, in the midst of my tears and excruciating pain and while holding a melting ice pack, I looked at David and said, "I won't be able to type tomorrow's Bible study!"

He looked at me and replied, "I know it hurts, but God has you! This is just the enemy distracting you. God is using you for the women in the Bible study, and you will not be defeated!"

* * *

1. Read Isaiah 43:1–7 (NKJV). What is the Lord speaking to you in this passage? Rewrite it in your own words, according to the revelation that is given to you.

"When you pass through the waters, I will be with you; And through the rivers, they shall not overflow you. When you walk through the fire, you shall not be burned, nor shall the flame scorch you. For I am the Lord your God, The Holy One of Israel, your Savior …" (Isaiah 43:2–3 NKJV).

I felt as though my hand was literally on fire from the inside out, and I am reminded that *when* (not if, but when) we experience trials the Lord will be there with us to protect and sustain us. "The river will not overflow you—and the flame will not scorch you." Each one of us is redeemed and chosen by God for a purpose. In this current season, one of my purposes is to fulfill His calling regarding this particular ministry; therefore, I *am* protected!

2. List any distractions that you experienced this week as you committed to purposely experience growth in the Lord.

~ In the midst of distractions, we have to keep our consciousness set on God, for when we recognize and acknowledge His presence and our purpose, it will change the outcome that was a set-up for defeat into victory.

Rejection vs. Election

1. Rejection—reflect on that word for a minute (set your timer for sixty seconds).

Rejection hurts because it causes us to experience a negative impact on our self-esteem. At some point in our lives (or maybe currently), each of us has experienced the emotional pain or anguish caused by rejection. Rejection can be experienced in various forms:

- Denied entry into a school, program, or social club
- Not obtaining a job opportunity that you were certain was created for you
- Stood up on a date or didn't receive a call-back from someone you thought was as interested as you were
- Negative experience(s) with coworkers or other worshipers at church
- Harsh criticism
- Dismissed by friends or family members
- Unrequited love
- Abusive relationship(s)
- Infidelity

Unlike physical pain, when you reflect on the memory of rejection you can experience those painful feelings all over again, as if it were happening now.

2. Write down key words to an experience (or experiences) in which you were rejected.

Regardless of whether your list refers to past or current hurt(s), put an X over each key word, and say the following prayer to release the power that has been given to the situation(s) or individual(s):

> Lord, you know what these crossed-off words represent. You know fully the situation(s) and the individual(s) involved that have caused me to feel as though I am less than, and at times it has affected my confidence in the woman that you have created and called me to be. So, Lord, I lift the words up to you right now in the name of Jesus, no longer giving them power over my past, over my present, or over my future; no longer giving them the power to allow me to believe that I am anything less than elite and elected in you. Amen.

* * *

For the past three days, it has been clearly identified that you are chosen, handpicked by God, redeemed for a purpose. How does that affect you? What is your response to such a statement? When you are told "You are chosen by God," do you believe it without a doubt, or do you question, "Why would God choose me?"

3.   We started yesterday's study with John 15:16. "You did not choose me but I chose you." Do you most often believe that you are elected by God or rejected by Him? What about you and/or your life makes you feel either way?

It is easy to believe that we may be rejected by God because of our personal sins, as well as question God's desire to choose "someone like me." But consider David, a man who God elected despite his sins. The Bible provides several accounts of David's life to illustrate a man who was both anointed and full with sin, a man God identified as having a heart for Him despite his being *imperfect*, a man who trusted and loved God and therefore pursued holiness through sincere repentance of his sins (although not without consequences). Thus, he received the redemption of God's grace.

Read 2 Samuel 11; 12:1–24.

4. What sin(s) did David commit in chapter 11?

5. Why did God send Nathan to David in chapter 12? What was God's response to David's repentance through Nathan?

6. What consequence(s) occurred in chapter 12 in response to David's sin?

7. How is God's grace illustrated in Samuel 12:24–25?

One thing that I take away from that passage is that God loves us despite ourselves. Regardless of our various sins (which may have a direct effect on us as well as on others), He gives us the opportunity to repent. Although many times we will experience painful consequences due to our sins, His "grace mercy and peace will be with you from God the Father, and from the Lord Jesus Christ the Son of the Father, in truth and love" (2 John 1:3).

8. In the space below and following page, write a prayer thanking God for being chosen by Him despite your sins. Ask Him to help you to fully believe, receive, and accept that you are elected and to cast out all previous or unforeseen thoughts of being rejected by Him. Take this time to also repent of any sins that you have not yet given up to the Lord. Thank Him for His grace, mercy, and ability to bring you peace and comfort even in the midst of consequences.

Jessica C. Jemmott, MA

Not without Purpose: First Group Session

It's day five—you've made it through week one. How was it? My prayer is that by the end of week six, we all will have experienced personal encounters with the Holy Spirit and gained a new freedom to walk in our purposes, according to the Lord. I am sure that many of us have already experienced new revelations this week, and that is great!

The activity from day four allowed us to witness an account from David's life in 2 Samuel 11 and 12 regarding sin, repentance, consequence, and God's grace. Scripture tells us repeatedly that when God removed Saul from his reign as king for not keeping God's commandment, God *chose* David as king because He was appointing "a man after His own heart and willing to do [His] will" (1 Samuel 13:24; Acts 13:22).

When God chooses you and appoints you to move or act according to His will, there is and always will be a *purpose* behind His choosing that is ultimately for His glory. His purpose in your life includes reaching others for either salvation or coming closer to Him, starting with you.

1. Identify something for which you know God is preparing you.

2. Read 1 Samuel 16. To what illustration in this chapter can you relate?

* * *

"The Lord doesn't see things the way you see them. People judge by outward appearance, but the Lord looks at the heart" (1 Samuel 16:7 NLT).

God sent Samuel to Bethlehem to anoint a son of Jesse as an appointed king. Neither Samuel nor Jesse expected God's chosen to be David, of all of Jesse's sons; at that time, David was a child.

(Note: as we gain a deeper understanding through the story of David of how God plans for His purpose long before our own acknowledgment, it's interesting to see how He sent Samuel to Bethlehem to anoint a child who later would become king. Sound familiar? I'll give you a hint: Mary, who was from Nazareth, traveled to Bethlehem, where Jesus was to be born; a child who would be named "King of kings and Lord of lords"; someone who, like David, also experienced rejection when others realized the anointing and purpose over his life.)

In question 1 you were asked to identify something for which God is preparing you. How are you allowing yourself to be moved toward that area in your life, spiritual walk, or purpose? You may not fully understand the calling or the purpose behind it right now, but understand that God has not mistakenly *chosen you*.

"For we are God's masterpiece. He has created us anew in Christ Jesus, so we can do the good things he planned for us long ago" (Ephesians 2:10 NLT).

Behind the Curtain

Synonyms for *behind the curtain* include in secret, in the dark, out of public view, and sub rosa

The Death of Jesus

From noon until three in the afternoon darkness came over all the land. About three in the afternoon Jesus cried out in a loud voice, "Eli, Eli,[a] lema sabachthani?" (which means "My God, my God, why have you forsaken me?"). When some of those standing there heard this, they said, "He's calling Elijah." Immediately one of them ran and got a sponge. He filled it with wine vinegar, put it on a staff, and offered it to Jesus to drink. The rest said, "Now leave him alone. Let us see if Elijah comes to save him." And when Jesus had cried out again in a loud voice, he gave up his spirit. At that moment the curtain of the temple was torn in two from top to bottom. The earth shook, the rocks split. (Matthew 27:45–51 NIV)

After reading Matthew 27:45–51 (and cross-referencing Luke 23:44–46 and Mark 15:33–38), ask yourself the following questions:

- What is the importance of the three hours of darkness?
- Why did Jesus say that God forsook him if He was aware of the prophecy?
- What is the significance of the curtain that was ripped?

"It was now about noon, and darkness came over the whole land until three in the afternoon, for the sun stopped shining" (Luke 23:44–45 NIV).

When Jesus was persecuted, tormented, and nailed to the cross, those were torturous brutalities against His physical body. He was aware of what was to come, but being nailed to the cross would not be the only thing to set Him apart.

For three hours (the number three spiritually represents God's purpose and will), an unexplained darkness came over the land, and for those three hours there was no word from the Lord. What happened in those three hours?

"But into the second [inner tabernacle, the Holy of Holies], only the high priest enters [and then only] once a year, and never without [bringing a sacrifice of] blood, which he offers [as a substitutionary atonement] for himself and for the sins of the people committed in ignorance" (Hebrews 9:7 AMP).

In Exodus, God appointed Moses to build the tabernacle (a sanctuary, a sacred place) with distinct instructions on its design and purpose. Part of the direct instruction from God included a veil, or curtain (Exodus 26:31–34). This curtain of tremendous height and superior breadth was placed to separate the two areas of the tabernacle: the Holy Place and the Holy of Holies, where the presence of God would enter. This curtain was symbolic of the separation of sin and man from the presence of God.

Only the appointed high priest was permitted to enter into the tabernacle and only once a year—on the Day of Atonement. On this appointed Day of Atonement, the high priest (one who is holy, set apart) would enter into the holy place to offer the sacrifice and atoning shed blood for himself and his family. Then into the Holy of Holies for the atonement of the sins of others with a blood sacrifice *in secret* (in the dark, out of public view, sub rosa). God's presence rested on the mercy seat, and anyone who entered into the Holy of Holies who was not appointed to do so would die (for the wages of sin is death).

"And at the ninth hour Jesus cried out with a loud voice, saying, 'Eloi, Eloi, lama sabachthani?' which is translated, 'My God, My God, why have You forsaken Me?'" (Mark 15:34 NKJV).

But the gift of God is eternal life in Christ Jesus our Lord. Jesus, being the high priest who was the *only* one without sin (for we are born into sin), has never experienced the spiritual persecutions of sin until this very moment.

Jesus has always known and experienced the presence of God. For those three hours of supernatural darkness and silence (a symbolic veil, or curtain—in secret in the dark, out of public view, sub rosa), Jesus suffered the wrath of God for the atonement of our sins, and for that He experienced anguish in the spirit that is beyond description or imagination.

Repeat the following aloud, and allow it to truly resonate with your spirit:

"Jesus suffered the wrath of God for the atonement of our sins, and for that He experienced anguish in the spirit that is beyond description or imagination."

"And Jesus cried out again with a loud voice, and yielded up His spirit. 51 Then, behold, the veil of the temple was torn in two from top to bottom; and the earth quaked, and the rocks were split" (Matthew 27:50–51 NKJV).

Just as the appointed priest entered into the Holy of Holies in atonement for the sins of the people with a blood sacrifice, Jesus was appointed by God to enter into the most holy presence as He yielded up His spirit. And for His sacrifice, the curtain was ripped!

The curtain did not merely fall down; rather, it was torn in two—the number two spiritually represents agreement and truth—from top to bottom, indicating that no man could have completed this task; rather, it was done by the hand of God.

You Now Have Access

For which of your sins did Jesus go behind the curtain?

In week one, day two, we discussed transparency in relationships. How did the idea of transparency affect you? Often we hide behind the curtain, only representing what others *expect* to see. You may say to yourself, "If they knew about _____, I would surely be judged"; "There's no way they would believe I am saved if they knew about _____"; or "No one will ever know about _____."

1. Take a moment to fill in your blanks below (no matter how many there are), and remember this is personal between you and the Lord. If you cannot be honest with yourself, how will you ever be transparent with Him?

Maybe the things you have listed are experiences, struggles, or sins of your past. Maybe they represent where you are currently. Wherever you stand, allow the Lord to meet you exactly there. The blessing in doing so is that when you face your own blanks, you no longer have to hide behind the curtain from Him or experience the burden of secrecy around others.

Your story is better than the character portrayed, for God will use you to encourage others, as well as allow them to witness His glory in yet another person who is not without sin but is simply redeemed!

2. Read Romans 8:1–11; Colossians 1:13–14, 22; Ephesians 1:13–14; Romans 8:38–39. What promises are revealed in these scriptures?

Are you having a difficult time accepting that you are loved and forgiven? If you find yourself questioning your salvation and the promises of God after reading the scriptures listed above, yet you desire the comfort of knowing that you are truly forgiven, then I urge to pray the following prayer of salvation:

Dear Lord, I know that I am not a sinner because I sin, but I sin because I am a sinner. Thank you, Jesus, for suffering on the cross for my sins. I now know what true love is because you were forsaken for a moment so that I could be in your presence forever. It is my desire to give you all of me, for your thoughts to become my thoughts, and for me to love myself and others as you love. I ask that you come into my life as my Savior, Lord, and friend. I am thankful that you hear my prayers and that my request for salvation has been immediately received and answered. In Jesus's name I pray. Amen."

    3.   If there are loved ones in your life who you are praying will come to know the Lord for themselves, write their names and pray the following prayer:

Dear Lord,

    I come to You on behalf of _____.

    I know that I cannot save them, but it is my prayer that while I share with them the love of Christ, I ask the Spirit to work that they may be drawn to Christ for salvation. I pray, Lord, that You may cause them to see their sins and that they may cry out to You in repentance. Show them, Father, the glories of Jesus as Savior, Lord, and King. In Jesus's name I pray. Amen.

"I have swept away your sins like a cloud. I have scattered your offenses like the morning mist. Oh, return to me, for I have paid the price to set you free" (Isaiah 44:22 NLT).

Seeking God

My four-year old, Jordan, is a very free and artistic child. While I enjoy exploring his creativity with him, David and I have had a hard time with his drawing pictures on the walls of our house. One night, David saw that Jordan had created yet another "masterpiece" on the wall—this time in marker! Of course his dad disciplined him with a stern voice for his actions and sent him to his room. We heard Jordan crying and mumbling quietly. I assumed he was talking to himself about his getting in trouble, but when I later asked what he was saying, he responded, "I was talking to Jesus. I said, 'I asked you to help me be good, and you just stood there and watched!'"

Imagine how difficult it was to keep our composure when such a response came from our four-year-old's mouth. After we quietly released our laughter, David used this as a teachable moment to explain God's free will: the power to make decisions on our own versus relying on God to predetermine our actions.

The innocence and honesty of my child reminded me that many of us have experienced those moments of seeking and questioning God, "Where were you when I needed you?" The Holy Spirit also uses those times as teachable moments. God allows us to make mistakes in order to learn and mature spiritually through repentance and the consequences received.

"I love those who love me, and those who seek me find me" (Proverbs 8:17 NIV).

God's desire is for us to *seek* him. At times we find ourselves in situations where we have used our free will and made the wrong choice. Then we look to Him, asking why He didn't remove us from the situation. If the Holy Spirit always rescued us from error before error was made, there would be no accountability, no lesson learned, and no need for redemption.

Jordan reminded us in his comment—"You just stood there and watched"—that even when we don't feel the Lord's presence or receive a direct response from Him, He is still there (to watch over us and protect us in the midst of our choices).

Record a time when you made a decision for which you later asked the Lord, "Why did you just stand there and watch?" What consequence(s) did you receive from that decision? What lesson did you learn?

Reflect on your experience above. Aren't you grateful that, even in that difficult lesson, He knows better than you yourself?

* * *

Read and complete the following scriptures:

"A man's heart prepares _____ way, But the Lord _____ his steps" (Proverbs 16:9, New King James Version).

"No _____ has overtaken you except such as is common to man; but God is _____ who will not allow you to be tempted beyond what you are able but with temptation will also make the way of _____ that you may be _____ to bear it" (1 Corinthians 10:13, New King James Version).

"_____ the Lord while He may be found; _____ upon Him while He is _____" (Isaiah 55:6, New King James Version).

"For the Lord is the _____ and wherever the Spirit of the Lord is, there is Freedom" (2 Corinthians 3:17, New Living Translation).

"For you have been called to live in _____ my brothers and sisters, But don't use your freedom to satisfy your sinful nature …" (Galatians 5:13, New Living Translation).

The next time you are faced with a decision regarding a *wrong* or *right* choice, remember that Satan's strategy is to target your free will. His desire is for you to disregard the freedom that God gives you and focus on the restrictions.

"The Lord God placed the man in the Garden of Eden to tend and watch over it. But the Lord God warned him, "You may freely eat the fruit of every tree in the garden—except the tree of the knowledge of good and evil. If you eat its fruit, you are sure to die" (Genesis 2:15–17 NLT).

Knowing God

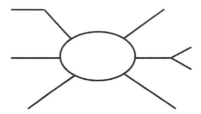

Do you recall using the "webbing brainstorming method" (as pictured above) in grade school? The teacher would instruct the student to identify the major topic in the center, while the links that connected the center identified supporting details about the topic. If you were to take this same idea to identify who God is to you, what would it look like? What would be your describing factors or supporting details?

- In the space below, complete a brainstorm web to identify the characteristics you recognize in God, according to your thoughts and personal relationship. (Be sure to include a link that includes any misconceptions that you've had.)

Read the following passages and list the personal characteristics of God presented in each:

1 John 4:8

Exodus 34:1–7

1 John 1:5

Galatians 5:22

Micah 7:18–19

Deuteronomy 4:24

Psalm 103:1–22

Each of us has a personal and distinct relationship with the Lord, according to our own interaction with Him through His Word and/or an experiential connection. How does your brainstorm web compare with God's characteristics in the previous passages?

Our almighty God is identified as a "jealous God" and one we should fear. The Lord has the power to make all things bow down to Him and cause them to "hear His majestic voice and make them see His arm coming down with raging anger and consuming fire with cloudburst, thunderstorm, and hail" (as in Isaiah 30; read it). We serve a God, however, who has chosen a personal and intimate way to give us insight into His character through individually *knowing Him.*

"If you really know me, you will know my Father as well. From now on, you do know him and have seen him" (John 14:7 NIV).

Just One Touch

I used to dance (minister) to the song "Let Me Touch You" by Kirk Franklin. Part of the lyrics are:

> When I'm lonely
> Let me touch You
> When I'm discouraged
> Let me touch You
> Like I never have before
> Lord, I need You more and more, Jesus
> Let me touch You and see if You are real

What Is in a Touch? Healing, Closeness, Intimacy, Trust

From infancy, touch has a significant impact on us. Psychologist Harry Harlow studied this impact in the 1960s. The study included baby monkeys, a wire "mother" that provided food, and a terrycloth "mother" that did not provide food. Harlow identified that the baby monkeys chose to spend significantly more time with the terrycloth mother than with the mother made of wire, despite the provision of food. This study, along with other experiments, allowed Harlow to identify that the deprivation of affection or touch may lead to psychological suffering, emotional distress, and/or death.

The Greek word for touch is *háptomai,* meaning to fasten to or lay hold of in a way that modifies or changes. Various accounts of individuals desiring a *touch* from the Lord or even to touch the hem of His garment are storied within the scriptures. When we read the accounts of Jesus's ability to heal with *just one touch*, it is powerful. Let us look deeper into the significance of His touch.

The Individuals

Read each scripture shown in italics:

Mark 8:22; *Matthew 8:2–3*; *Matthew 20:34*; *Mark 5:24–34*. Blindness, leprosy, issue of blood—what do these individuals have in common? They were shunned, considered as unclean, and probably were untouched by anyone for quite some time. Can you imagine the emotional pain that accompanied the physical agony for these individuals who desired a touch from the Lord?

His Garment—*Luke 8:40–49*

This passage provides another account of the woman with the issue of blood. According to the scripture, this particular woman had been experiencing a medical concern for twelve years, and no doctor or healer had been able to assist her. Jesus was walking through a packed crowd, being touched by many due to the lack of space, but this woman was so determined that she made it through the crowd, even in her weakness, believing if she just touched His garment, she would be healed.

In ancient Israel the men wore tunics that had four corners known as *tallit*, with tassels or fringes called the *tzitzit*. The tzitzit was a reminder to fulfill God's commandments for the man who wore them. They hung on the four corners of the tallit, which everyone could see, as a reminder to walk according to the law of God, in a path of righteousness.

Malachi 4:2 identifies "healing in his wings." The Hebrew word for wings is *kanaph*, representing the corners of the garment. When we read this passage with historical understanding, it is now implied that this woman, not wanting to be identified or noticed due to her "uncleanliness," had great faith that touching the tzitzit of Jesus's tallit would bring healing. It was not His clothing that healed her but her faith.

His Hands

Several Bible scholars and commentaries question the belief that Jesus was a carpenter. *Matthew 13:55* and *Mark 6:3* are the only references regarding Jesus being the "son of a carpenter" (Joseph) and being a carpenter Himself. Jewish custom required fathers to teach their sons the trade of the father when the sons were age twelve, which is why Jesus may have taken on this skill.

The Greek word for carpenter, *tektón*, also means "craftsman." Regardless of whether Jesus was a carpenter or a craftsman and whether He built with wood or stones (also questioned due to the era and location), Jesus was raised in a working-class home and had experience working with His hands. Therefore, as a man who was living in a time where His hands were the "machinery" for such a trade or skill, they may not have been the softest hands to the touch.

But oh how *gentle* was just one touch, and oh how *powerful* was just one touch! These hands surrendered themselves in prayer to God the Father. These hands modified crafts and changed the lives of many. A touch from these hands was sought with steadfast faith. And these hands were pierced and bruised for our iniquities. What would you do for *just one touch*?

- Write a personal prayer, thanking the Lord for your experience(s) with His touch.

"For He had healed many, with the result that all those who had afflictions pressed around Him in order to touch Him" (Mark 3:10 NASB).

The Perfect Fit

A few months after I delivered our second son, Caleb, I couldn't wait to get back into my pre-pregnancy jeans. Every other week or so I would pull my favorite pair of blue jeans out of the closet and try them on to see what progress (if any) I had made. And each time, I said to myself, "If only they would go past my thighs!" Finally, one morning as I was getting dressed, with both of my boys in my room (the older one cheering Mommy on), I again pulled down my favorite pair of jeans and slipped each leg on one at time. To my surprise, they continued to move up past my thighs and over my behind. I zipped and buttoned, without the acrobatic skills that it previously had taken. *It was a perfect fit!* I was excited!

I began to dance around as I continued to get ready for the day. And then it happened—the most devastating noise I could hear. My excitement quickly changed to dejection as I heard, in slow motion, *s-l-i-i-t-ch*—the sound of my jeans ripping at the seams over my thighs.

Doctors say your body will never be the same after pregnancy. This is not always in reference to weight (or the shifting of weight, in my case) but the many physical and emotional changes that occur that others may not see right away. This particular pair of jeans, which were already contoured to my previous shape like memory foam, with seams that were stretched and molded to fit me, appeared to be a *perfect fit*. But post-pregnancy, after the physical and internal changes to my body, what appeared to fit no longer did. Before I knew it, the changes that were only evident to me became evident to my four-year-old who witnessed the whole thing.

"Therefore, if anyone is in Christ, he is a new creation; old

things have passed away; behold, all things have become new"
(2 Corinthians 5:17 NKJV).

When Christ is in you, not only is He working *on* you spiritually but *through* you for others to witness Him as well. Activities you once enjoyed are no longer enjoyable; certain friends no longer share commonality with you; conversations begin to change; your posts on social media begin to change; and, to some, you may even start to "look different." You no longer fit in.

1.   Think back to when you were first saved (whether it was fifty years ago or a week ago), where were you once a perfect fit but change (either immediately or gradually) began to take effect.

Maybe you've noticed a recent change in your life spiritually. Have you felt the Holy Spirit moving you into a closer relationship with the Lord?

2.   It's been two weeks since the start of your commitment toward spiritual growth through this Bible study. What personal changes have you already seen?

It was difficult for me to not only accept that I needed a new wardrobe but that my favorite pair of jeans were destroyed. But what is the point of forcing yourself to fit into something that is too small? Not only are you uncomfortable, but it does not look good on you. That is how it is spiritually as well. When the Holy Spirit is working through you, you are no longer comfortable with where you once fit, and others begin to notice that something is different about you. For some, the difference may draw them closer, as they want to know the change for themselves. Others may pull away.

Your social construct either has changed, is beginning to change, or will change. Be prayerful during these moments of transition in your walk with Christ. It is during these times that you may feel discomfort in changing or may not relate in situations where you were once the *perfect fit*. It is difficult to experience, but rest assured that the Lord is preparing you for more.

Your spiritual growth is busting at the seams!

Fearfully and Wonderfully Made

It is no secret that many times we are our own biggest critics, whether it is based on our individual looks, personalities, life accomplishments, or skills. Despite the positive or negative opinions of others or validated facts, we nevertheless tend to find the flaw before the splendor.

Acceptance of self can be a tough task, but you must begin to see yourself as the Lord sees you. This week may be one of the most difficult for you, as it will challenge you to confront the one individual who tends to get in the way of your ability to receive a blessing, provision, or direction from the Lord—*you.*

For you created my inmost being; you knit me together in my mother's womb. I praise you because I am fearfully and wonderfully made; your works are wonderful, I know that full well. My frame was not hidden from you when I was made in the secret place, when I was woven together in the depths of the earth. Your eyes saw my unformed body; all the days ordained for me were written in your book before one of them came to be. (Psalm 139:13–16 NIV)

During the first group session after week one (in accordance with the Leader Guide), you had the opportunity to introduce yourself during an icebreaker activity with the task of sharing one thing that you *like* about yourself. Write your answer/statement.

It is my prayer that by the end of this week the one thing that was difficult for you to identify will become a list of things that you not only *like* but *love* about yourself.

Dear heavenly Father, You have created me comparable to no other. You knew every detail of my being while You were yet forming me in my mother's womb. Lord, there are things that I have allowed to enter my thoughts or my life, such as (insecurities, self-hate, self-doubt—*circle those that apply*) that hinder me from fully seeing the splendor of Your creation. Lord, help me to accept every good thing that You have done in me and deny every negative seed that has been planted. Lord, I realize that my inability to love me how You love me and see me how You see me may lead to and/or has caused me to experience (depression, unforgiveness, jealousy, self-harm, anxiety, bitterness, intimidation, addiction—*circle those that apply*), and I am standing here ready to be free from the bondage of being held mentally and spiritually captive. I stand here in need of You, Lord, to do a work in me that would allow me to see the change both spiritually and outwardly. I am ready to love me, Lord, for I know and am willing to acknowledge that I am fearfully and wonderfully made. Amen.

Mirror, Mirror

Living in a time where the selfie (a photograph you take of yourself) has become a societal norm, we are often critical about what the camera captures. How many times have you taken a selfie, but it took several shots before you were satisfied with what you saw, or you decided not to post it for others to see because you were never satisfied? While some individuals can't get enough of the digital mirror, others refrain from looking at their reflections at all costs. Where do you fall in?

Mirrors and photographs can be intimidating to the individual who finds it difficult to see her own outward beauty, the individual who is critical of herself because she identifies perceived flaws before recognizing the splendor of God's creation.

1. Have you ever been guilty of picking yourself apart in the mirror? What have you said about yourself? (Check all that apply)

_____I'm ugly.

_____I'm fat.

_____I'm too skinny.

_____I'm too old.

_____I hate the way I look.

_____I would look better if _____ (fill in the blank).

_____No one will ever find me attractive.

_____I'm not good enough.

_____I'm not smart enough.

_____I have no talent.

_____Everything would be better if I'd never been born [or if I disappeared].

2. From where have you derived these self-inflicting statements? Are they someone else's words? Are they the result of you comparing yourself to others?

Document your recollection of the initiation and progression over time of the statements that you checked above.

"He chose to give birth to us by giving us his true word. And we, out of all creation, became his prized possession" (James 1:18 NLT).

My sister, know that you are made in the image of God, according to Genesis 1:27. God has created *you*. Don't you know that there is no mistake in His creation?

Satan wants to plant the seed of doubt in your mind. He wants you to be insecure about your looks, your abilities, and your purpose here on earth so that you will question God and doubt His ability to use you. If Satan can get you to be insecure about your looks, you will believe that God spent less time on you and *more time* on others. If Satan can get you to question your abilities and talents, then you will doubt God's desire to use those abilities in your natural and spiritual purposes. Don't be distracted by doubt.

3. Stare into a mirror and be enamored with what you see. Reverse the self-inflicting statements that you checked above into positive statements. (Document your reaction to this exercise.)

What you see in the mirror ought to reflect your acknowledgment of God's perfect creation, so that you may reflect His love to others when they see you. You are His prized possession!

Write and repeat the prayer from week three, day one.

True Identity

At the age of eighteen I experienced what some might label as an "identity crisis." For the first time I was faced with acknowledging a part of me that was known to only a few members of my family, a part of me that had caused me to question my identity since I was a young child. It was a part of me that led me to explore what my identity in Christ really meant at the age of twelve by labeling myself as "God's child." For the first time, I faced the man who was not my dad but my biological father; along with his wife and daughter.

Within three weeks of meeting him and his family and hoping to find a connection with someone with whom I could identify regarding my appearance, I left for college; he went into a coma, and three weeks later he passed away. "What was the meaning of all of this, Lord?" I asked.

As a child I would question my appearance in the presence of my parents. I would cry out to God, "Why does my hair look like this and my complexion like this?" In an attempt to Band-Aid the situation, my family (those both aware and unaware of the truth of the matter) would explain that I got my looks from my maternal grandmother or my aunt on this side or a distant relative. However, no one knew or understood the damage that this would cause my ability to experience self-acceptance.

My freshman year of college was when the deadliest tsunami in history took place: the 2004 Indian Ocean tsunami. A ministry team at my university decided to plan a short-term overseas mission trip to assist with the aftereffects of the tsunami. When the announcement was made about the trip, I felt overwhelmingly compelled to go. This was new for me. I'd always wanted to travel, but I hadn't considered a foreign mission. I had no passport, no visa, no money—the list went on and on. But in that moment, the Holy Spirit clearly stated, "Do as I am telling you, for I will provide!"

My experiences while in India could be another book on its own, but it was during this ten-day period while in Chennai, Tamil Nadu, and nearby villages that the Lord began to open my eyes, and I saw part of His plan. It was because of my appearance—my hair, my complexion, my eyes—that I was accepted and received by every individual that we came across. At times this occurred before anyone else in my small group was accepted. Imagine—me, an American girl from Coatesville, Pennsylvania, being used by God to communicate the love of Christ to individuals who spoke strictly Tamil. But He did it! For God's love transcends all understanding and allows communication to manifest from heart to heart.

Upon my return, I received an on-campus job working at the Center for Multicultural Enrichment as a program coordinator for multicultural competency through special events, on and off campus. Having this position, I became known as "the poster child of all nations" among coworkers and friends. It was during this time that I reflected on past and current experiences, and I realized that the Lord makes no mistakes. God created me with His purpose in mind—I'd been given the ability to approach any people of any culture, race, ethnicity, or walk of life for His kingdom. Through these experiences, I realized and accepted that my identity does not rely on who my parents are, my family, or my appearance. My true identity is in Christ

"He says, 'It is too light a thing that you should be my servant to raise up the tribes of Jacob and to bring back the preserved of Israel; I will make you as a light for the nations, that my salvation may reach to the end of the earth'" (Isaiah 49:6 ESV).

- This journey of self-acceptance continued several years after the experiences that I have documented. The process allowed me to seek truth and be released from strongholds and shame. What does your journey to reveal your true identity look like?

"So God created man in His own image; in the image of God He created him; male and female He created them" (Genesis 1:27 NKJV).

"For we are His workmanship [His own master work, a work of art], created in Christ Jesus [reborn from above—spiritually transformed, renewed, ready to be used] for good works, which God prepared [for us] beforehand [taking paths which He set], so that we would walk in them [living the good life which He prearranged and made ready for us]" (Ephesians 2:10 AMP).

Personal Reflection

I remember, like it was yesterday, sitting up on my bed in the middle of the night in the dorm, freshman year, literally crying out to the Lord, *"Why?"* Why did God allow these moments of give and take to happen? Why was I given a moment to finally meet this man and his family after all of the walls I'd come up against in the past, only for him to be taken away? Why, with *all* that I'd experienced and seen in my life, was yet another burden presented? *Why?*

And for the first time, I felt the Lord's presence in that moment as I'd *never* felt it previously. As I cried out, His arms wrapped around me, holding me and comforting me, preparing me for the blessings to come. The following morning, I apologized to my roommate for the disturbance I'd caused that night—she had no clue I caused a "disturbance"!

That year, I gained a relationship with a brother and sister, nieces and nephews, aunts and uncles I'd never met before. That year, the Lord used me to encourage others who experienced loss. That year, my dad told me that he loves me. That year, I grew closer in my personal relationship with the Lord. That year, the self-proclaimed name "God's child" meant more than ever before.

For God's love transcends all understanding!

I Knew You When

At this point in the study, it has been identified that you are *chosen* with a *purpose*. You are continuing to *seek God's presence,* while desiring His *touch*, and you understand that your *true identity* is in Him. But do you have the "I knew you when …" people in your life?

Each of us has a "pre-salvation" story, for you were born a sinner, and after you were saved, you are now perfect—*not!*

It will always be God's grace and love that sustains us. However, the enemy knows our pasts, our struggles, and our weaknesses, and he knows just who to use to push our buttons. Many times it's the individuals to whom we are closest or those to whom we are ministering with our own actions and reactions.

The individuals that say, "Hm-m-m, I knew you when you use to do [this]" or "when you use to say [that]." Don't get caught being less than perfect around them now, because they are the individuals who *question* your salvation or imply that you are not a "real Christian" or a "good Christian" (terms that I wish would be deleted) or that you have any anointing in the Holy Spirit at all.

Do not be dismayed by such judgment; it is a plot of the enemy. As individuals who are redeemed by love and grace, it is always our desire to live a life that glorifies God, but we are called by God to bear good fruit, not produce it, for He produces the fruit.

"By this my Father is glorified, that you bear much fruit and so prove to be my disciples" (John 15:8 ESV).

"But the fruit of the Spirit is love, joy, peace, patience, kindness, goodness, faithfulness, gentleness, self-control; against such things there is no law" (Galatians 5:22–23 ESV).

I am thankful that the scriptures are filled with accounts of individuals who, like me, were far from perfect, both before and after being used by God. Did you catch that? God can use *you*.

4. Choose *three* of the passages below and record on the following page characteristics with which you identify and how God has used you, despite your actions. (Mark this page so you can go back and read/study each passage later.)

- Jacob was a liar (Genesis 27).
- David had an affair (2 Samuel 11).
- Paul was a murderer (Acts 8:1–5; 9:1–2; Galatians 1:13; 1 Corinthians 15:9–10).
- Miriam was a gossip and was jealous and envious (Numbers 12).
- Jeremiah was depressed (Jeremiah 15:18; 20:7).
- Elijah was depressed and wanted to die (1 Kings 19).
- Noah was a drunk (Genesis 9:20–27).
- Peter was impulsive (John 18:10).
- Martha was a worrier (Luke 10).
- Gideon was afraid (Judges 6:1–32).
- Rahab was a prostitute (Joshua 6:17–25).
- Jonah ran from God (Jonah 1:3).
- Peter denied Christ (Luke 22:54–62).
- Disciples fell asleep (Matthew 26:40).
- The Samaritan woman divorced five times (John 4:3–42).

The next time you are faced with an individual who questions your salvation or anointing, remember that God uses ordinary people to do extraordinary things, according to His will. It is through Him that we are qualified. Be not in bondage of the perceptions of others.

Do Not Pass Judgment on One Another

"As for the one who is weak in faith, welcome him, but not to quarrel over opinions" (Romans 14:1 ESV).

A Love Letter

You are altogether beautiful, my love; there is no flaw in you … You have captivated my heart, my sister, my bride; you have captivated my heart with one glance of your eyes, with one jewel of your necklace. How beautiful is your love, my sister, my bride! How much better is your love than wine, and the fragrance of your oils than any spice! (Song of Solomon 4:7, 9–10)

Have you ever written, received, or desired a love letter? What did it mean to you? How did you feel, or what was your desired feeling as you read or sent a love letter? Regardless of the intended recipient—a lover, a family member, a friend—it was written to identify how you genuinely cherish, relish, honor, and care for another.

What Is Love?

"Love is patient and kind. Love is not jealous or boastful or proud or rude. It does not demand its own way. It is not irritable, and it keeps no record of being wronged. It does not rejoice about injustice but rejoices whenever the truth wins out. Love never gives up, never loses faith, is always hopeful, and endures through every circumstance. Prophecy and speaking in unknown languages and special knowledge will become useless. But love will last forever!" (1 Corinthians 13:4–8 NLT).

1. At the beginning of this week you were challenged to identify what you like about yourself, with the goal of being able to recognize what you *love* about you. Meditate on 1 Corinthians 13:4–8, and then write a love letter to yourself.

"So we have come to know and to believe the love that God has for us. God is love, and whoever abides in love abides in God, and God abides in him" (1 John 4:16 ESV).

2.   God's love for you is continually identified. Now is your time to express your love for Him. Write an intimate love letter to God.

"My beloved is mine and I am His ..." (Song of Solomon 2:16).

But the Greatest of These Is Love

In week three we discussed love—loving God, loving self, and what love is—but let's not neglect the instruction from God to love others.

Before we move forward, take a moment to think about several things that God has commanded of you, and write them down.

1.

2.

3.

At any point in receiving the instruction (whether scriptural or personal direction), was it easy? Were you able to accomplish the instruction immediately without any hesitation or any effort and without prayer and guidance?

More than likely you answered no in regard to at least one of the instructions. If loving others was meant to be easy, the instruction to do so would not appear in the scriptures so frequently and urgently.

In relation to loving others, the Bible identifies *others* in the scripture as individuals, including those in relationships and marriage, children, family, friends, enemies, and strangers.

As long as you have lived and experienced life, I am certain there have been times where any of the above "others" have made it hard for you to love them, and that is why we are commanded to do so. "God is _____" (1 John 4:8).

What do you learn from the following scriptures? Fill in the blanks.

"Jesus said to him, 'You shall _____ the Lord your God with all your heart, with all your soul, and with all your mind.' This is the first and great commandment. And the second is like it: 'You shall _____ your neighbor as yourself'" (Matthew 22:37–39, NKJV).

"Therefore _____ the stranger, for you were strangers in the land of Egypt" (Deuteronomy 10:19, NKJV).

"Dear children, let us not _____ with words or speech but with actions and in truth" (1 John 3:18, NIV).

"Hatred stirs up conflict, but _____ covers over all wrongs" (Proverbs 10:12, NIV).

"And over all these virtues put on _____, which binds them all together in perfect unity" (Colossians 3:14, NIV).

"Husbands, _____ your wives, just as Christ _____ the church and gave himself up for her; … However, each one of you also must _____his wife as he _____ himself, and the wife must respect her husband" (Ephesians 5:25, 33, NIV).

"Dear friends, let us _____ one another, for _____ comes from God. Everyone who _____ has been born of God and knows God" (1 John 4:7, NIV).

"Above all, _____ each other deeply, because love covers over a multitude of sins" (1 Peter 4:8, NIV).

"Be completely humble and gentle; be patient, bearing with one another in _____" (Ephesians 4:2, NIV).

"_____ does no harm to a neighbor. Therefore _____ is the fulfillment of the law" (Romans 13:10, NIV).

"The second is this: '_____ your neighbor as yourself.' There is no commandment greater than these." (Mark 12:31, NIV).

"_____ must be sincere. Hate what is evil; cling to what is good" (Romans 12:9, NIV).

"But _____ your enemies, and do good, and lend, expecting nothing in return, and your reward will be great, and you will be sons of the Most High, for he is kind to the ungrateful and the evil" (Luke 6:35, ESV).

Think about the individual that you may find it difficult to truly love, not just with words but with action and truth (according to 1 John 3:18), and sincerely give it to the Lord in prayer each day this week.

"And now abide faith, hope, love, these three; but the greatest of these is love"
(1 Corinthians 13:13 NKJV).

Unrequited Love

- ○ A marriage falling apart
- ○ A child chasing the shadow of an uninvolved parent
- ○ A parent seeking restoration with his or her prodigal child
- ○ A man or woman pining after another for intimacy
- ○ A lonely individual desiring platonic affection from one to be called friend

The commonality among each of these individuals and very personal experiences is *unrequited love*—a love that is one-sided and not reciprocated.

In week one, day four, unrequited love was included in the various methods in which individuals experience rejection. Rejection hurts our pride. It can make us emotional or numb to our emotions, and it leaves scars. Rejection can cause those who are hurting to hurt others.

Why?

We have all heard the term "love hurts." However, it is not love that hurts us, for again, God is love (1 John 4:8). It is our pride that becomes battered in the experiences of rejection and neglect of those from whom we seek validation and recognition—those to whom we express our love but who continue to hurt us in the process.

"But if you love those who love you, what credit is that to you? For even sinners love those who love them" (Luke 6:32 NKJV).

It was stated on day one of this week that if it was easy to love others, the instruction to do so would not appear in the Bible so frequently and urgently. I believe that greatly includes experiences of unrequited love.

God Himself experienced unrequited love many times, according to the scripture. Can you imagine—the one who created love, the one who *is* love all-abiding not receiving love? It happens every day, but if we look back at scriptural accounts regarding His responses, we will see that while at times they were very harsh and frightening—and I'm thankful that it wasn't me experiencing His wrath—His love always prevails.

Great examples of God's unfailing redemptive love, despite the rejection of others, include:

- The promises of Israel in the book of Hosea
- The story of Noah and the ark in Genesis 5:32–10:1
- The Prodigal Son in Luke 15:11–32
- Saul of Tarsus in Acts 9
- The people of Ninevah in the book of Jonah

Choose two of the stories provided as examples of God's unfailing love, and explore the rejection, the response, and God's demonstration of redeeming love. (Read the stories you did not choose later for your personal study.) Write your reflections in the space provided below and the page that follows.

"And above all things have fervent love for one another, for 'love will cover a multitude of sins'" (1 Peter 4:8 NKJV).

Reflections

Love Is Stronger than Pride

All too common are the stories and experiences that individuals face when another's wrongdoing causes negative effects of *pride* to creep in and reign over the ability to express unconditional love, or *agape* love.

"By pride comes nothing but strife" (Proverbs 13:10 NKJV).

Pride is defined as "a high or inordinate opinion of one's own dignity, importance, merit, or superiority, whether as cherished in the mind or as displayed in bearing, conduct, etc."[1]

• Identify a personal experience where pride caused you to allow another individual's failure to keep you in mental or spiritual bondage because your worth was devalued.

Pride has several definitions, but today's study refers to pride that causes conflict. There are two sides to this form of pride—one from the offender and the other from the offended. Consider the account of Diotrephes.

Read 3 John 1:9–11.

---

[1] Definition provided by Dictionary.com

Who is the offender?

How did he exhibit pride?

What is apostle John's instruction to the offended?

I encourage you as John did: do not imitate the evil behavior or action that comes against you from others in an attempt to justify your own pride; rather, respond with love and forgiveness.

* * *

Are you the Diotrephes among others? Ask yourself these things:

1. Do your interests in self outweigh the needs and feelings of others?
2. Do you expect to be appreciated or esteemed at all times?
3. Are you consistently suspicious, jealous, and/or envious of others?
4. Do you respond with slights rather than receive or forgive criticism?
5. Do you demand agreement with your own views?
6. Do you sulk if people are not grateful to you for your service?

If you relate to these characteristics, then I urge you to be God-centered rather than self-centered! The core of living a Christlike life is loving others as He did—selflessly.

"When pride comes, then comes disgrace, but with humility comes wisdom" (Proverbs 11:2 NIV).

What Is Love without Forgiveness?

As if meeting my biological father and experiencing his passing just weeks later wasn't enough to add into my overflowing cup of rejections, I also was dealing with various hurts from several individuals in my life at the same time—hurts that caused me to feel bitterness and anger toward them. I distinctly remember attending campus church during my freshman year one evening, and the pastor said the following: "Not forgiving others is like drinking poison and expecting the other person to get sick—you're only hurting yourself."

Consider the warning Jesus gave in the following scripture for us to prevent putting ourselves in the position to be unforgiving or to not fully receive forgiveness.

"For if you forgive other people when they sin against you, your heavenly Father will also forgive you. But if you do not forgive others their sins, your Father will not forgive your sins" (Matthew 6:14–15 NIV).

We are provided with a great example of unrequited love, pride, and *forgiveness* in the story of Joseph.

Read Genesis 37:1–50:26.

1. How did Joseph experience unrequited love?

2. How did Joseph's brothers betray him?

3. How was Joseph used to extend grace to his brothers?

4. How was Joseph and his family blessed by his ability to reconcile and forgive his brothers?

Joseph's experiences are an example to us that even in the most difficult of situations, we are called to express love and forgiveness and allow God to handle the rest (Genesis 50:19–21).

"Bear with each other and forgive one another if any of you has a grievance against someone. Forgive as the Lord forgave you. And over all these virtues put on love, which binds them all together in perfect unity" (Colossians 3:13–14 NIV).

I encourage you to accept the apology that has yet to be received. Don't give the individual or the apology power over your ability to forgive. We desire an apology because it acknowledges that our hurts exist, but know that if you do not receive an apology from someone who has wronged you, that doesn't validate your worth, for your worth is in Christ.

The Hill

On the hill there's a cross
On the cross there is blood for me, for me
Still have the power
Wonderful power
To heal our diseases
To cover our weakness
On the hill there's a cross
On the cross there is blood for me

—Travis Greene, "The Hill"

Of all of the examples of love and forgiveness provided in the scriptures, the greatest example of unfailing redemptive love is Christ Himself and the fulfillment of prophecy on the cross.

"When they came to the place called the Skull, they crucified him there, along with the criminals—one on his right, the other on his left. Jesus said, 'Father, forgive them, for they do not know what they are doing.' And they divided up his clothes by casting lots" (Luke 23:33–34 NIV).

The Gospels of Matthew, Mark, Luke, and John give the accounts of the Crucifixion of Christ through detailed descriptions of the humiliation, the mocking, the physical and verbal abuse, the suffering, and His death.

Reading about the Crucifixion is enough for us to understand that God loves us so much that He gave His only Son (John 3:16) to die on the cross for our sins. The coming, the death, the resurrection, and the return of Christ are prophecies that are identified from the beginning of God's Word. One of the most amazing prophecies that we are provided is a first-person account of Jesus's direct experience of what was happening to Him through the prophetic word of David in Psalms 22, written a thousand years prior to the Crucifixion taking place!

Before you move forward, ask the Lord for His touch and to speak to you through the reading of His Word. Allow yourself to receive whatever you are in search of and whatever you desire to be released from through this week of *love and forgiveness.*

Read Psalm 22.

1.   In what way has your understanding of God's love for you developed or increased through this reading and the assignments of this week?

2.   What has the Holy Spirit exposed to you regarding your ability to demonstrate agape love, reject pride, and bestow forgiveness on others in your own life?

Imitating Christ's Humility

"Therefore if you have any encouragement from being united with Christ, if any comfort from his love, if any common sharing in the Spirit, if any tenderness and compassion, then make my joy complete by being like-minded, having the same love, being one in spirit and of one mind. Do nothing out of selfish ambition or vain conceit. Rather, in humility value others above yourselves" (Philippians 2:1–3 NIV).

"Bloody and beautiful, bloody and beautiful, bloody and beautiful hill."
—Travis Greene

Beautiful Liar

The Fall

> Now the serpent was more crafty than any of the wild animals the Lord God had made. He said to the woman, "Did God really say, 'You must not eat from any tree in the garden?" The woman said to the serpent, "We may eat fruit from the trees in the garden, but God did say, "You must not eat fruit from the tree that is in the middle of the garden, and you must not touch it, or you will die.' You will not certainly die, "the serpent said to the woman, "For God knows that when you eat from it your eyes will be opened, and you will be like God, knowing good and evil." (Genesis 3:1–8 NIV)

What do we know about Satan? According to the scriptures, he is many things. Satan (also known as the devil and the evil one) is a liar, a manipulator, a murderer—the list goes on. With identities like those, how is that we are conned by him repeatedly? It's because Satan, who is the ruler of darkness, disguises himself as an angel of light.

"And no wonder, for Satan himself masquerades as an angel of light" (2 Corinthians 11:14 NIV).

How befitting that the one who was cursed by God and cast out of heaven—because he allowed his beauty, his splendor, and his anointing to cause him to fall, due to his conceit and attempt to be like the Most High—now uses his influence to entice others to become like him by deceiving people into believing they can be above God, that they don't need God, and that they themselves can be like God.

Satan, ruler of the darkness of this world, is often portrayed as an evil, dark, fear-provoking being. He can be those things, but we must be mindful and understand that this is not how he presents himself, and that's for a very strategic reason.

Think about it: we turn away from evil images. We refrain from going down dark alleys alone. We are reminded in scripture to fear not, so to what do we turn? Light. Therefore, he wants you to believe that he is an angel of light, that he speaks truth, that he is loving, and that he has power. He wants to be portrayed has having the characteristics of God so that you will be deceived by him and be diverted from the path set for you by God alone.

Satan does not want to be called out. When you acknowledge what he truly is—a liar—he works harder to deceive you. I ask that you be especially mindful of protecting yourself spiritually, mentally, and physically this week, through prayer and reading of the Word, as well as specifically asking the Holy Spirit to guide you on how to pray daily during this particular study topic.

"He was a murderer from the beginning, not holding to the truth, for there is no truth in him. When he lies, he speaks his native language, for he is a liar and the father of lies" (John 8:44 NIV).

Week 5—Day 2

Stronger

"Be sober [well balanced and self-disciplined], be alert and cautious at all times. That enemy of yours, the devil, prowls around like a roaring lion [fiercely hungry], seeking someone to devour" (1 Peter 5:8 AMP).

Four years into my marriage, everything appeared to be going well. David and I were trying to conceive a second child, I was completing my master's degree in professional counseling, and ministry opportunities were growing for both of us. Then … the enemy found a perfect opportunity to creep into our marriage and attack us in an attempt to divert our paths and promises in the Lord, both individually and as a couple.

This was a time when I experienced one of the worst oppositions of my life. It affected my emotional and psychological well-being, my marriage, and my spiritual walk. The enemy does not know our thoughts or the promises that God has for us, but he *is* aware of those who are determined to engage in living an anointed life. He is cognizant of where our pressure points are. He knows our past and is interested in what seeds he can plant to distract us. When he sees that we are nearing the fulfillment of God's promise for our lives, that's when he attacks!

After attacking David, the enemy saw fit to strike at what was now a vulnerable time for me. The Holy Spirit gave me dreams and warnings, but rather than protecting myself and running away from the enemies trap, I ran right into it, embracing the lure of the lion. (I have never felt so close and yet so far from God at the same time.) I was so confused by the enemy that I allowed him to make me believe that I could be bound by my circumstances and past abuse. Although

I had godly counsel encamped around me, I sought justification from where I knew I would receive it. I strayed from the voice of the Holy Spirit, and I allowed the enemy to fool me into believing that this situation was "too big" for God.

The Holy Spirit provided guidance so that I could be alert, yet I ignored the warning. But God is merciful! I will never forget the day I received freedom as I laid it all on the altar and gave my situation to the Lord. It was then that the chains were broken.

Thank you, Lord, for your grace, for there was a lesson in your conviction. My marriage is stronger because of it.

"You meant evil against me but God meant it for good" (Genesis 50:20).

Satan's tactics include temptation, lies and half-truths, deception, intimidation, fear, theft, and murder.

    1.   Locate two occasions in the Bible where Satan used any of the above tactics.

    2.   Identify your personal experience when you were under attack by the enemy but became stronger in the Lord because of it.

"But the Lord is faithful, and He will strengthen you [setting you on a firm foundation] and will protect and guard you from the evil one" (2 Thessalonians 3:3 AMP).

I Know I've Been Changed

Shame corrodes the very part of us that believes we are capable of change.
—Brené Brown

Is there someone in your life (or path) who constantly reminds you of your past mistakes, your less-than-perfect decision-making skills, your *multiple* failures? Is there an individual who causes you to feel burdened with personal shame and guilt?

"Forget the former things; do not dwell on the past. See, I am doing a new thing!" (Isaiah 43:18–19 NIV).

We are reminded several times in the Word that when we become believers and followers of Christ by acknowledging that He is Lord, in Him we are a *new creation*. But your biggest enemy, Satan, wants to ignite a spiritual warfare within your mind—one that causes you to feel guilt and to be bounded by shame. You have been forgiven of the sins of your past, and as a believer your sins today and those to come no longer have any bearing on your salvation. However, Satan deceives you into false guilt in an attempt to cause you to refuse Christ's atonement for your sins.

You are *redeemed* through the blood of Christ and receive the forgiveness of sins, according to the riches of His grace (Ephesians 1:7). God's kindness and mercy is intended to lead you to repentance. Satan brings upon guilt and shame to cause you to feel unworthy of God's grace, separating you from your desire to be intimate with God and the confidence you have received in knowing that *you are redeemed.*

Read and complete the following scriptures:

"Therefore, if anyone is in Christ, he is a _____. The old has passed away; behold, the new has come" (2 Corinthians 5:17, ESV).

"To put off your old self, which belongs to your former manner of life and is corrupt through deceitful desires, and to be _____ in the spirit of your minds, and to put on the _____, created after the likeness of God in true righteousness and holiness" (Ephesians 4:22–24, ESV).

"I will sprinkle clean water on you, and you shall be clean from all your uncleannesses, and from all your idols I will cleanse you. And I will give you a new heart, and a _____ I will put within you. And I will remove the heart of stone from your flesh and give you a heart of flesh. And I will put my Spirit within you, and cause you to walk in my statutes and be careful to obey my rules" (Ezekiel 36:25–27, ESV).

"Remember not _____, nor consider the things of old. Behold, I am doing a _____; now it springs forth, do you not perceive it? I will make a way in the wilderness and rivers in the desert" (Isaiah 43:18–19, ESV).

"As far as the east is from the west, so far has he _____ our transgressions from us" (Psalm 103:12, NIV).

"You will again have compassion on us; you will tread our sins underfoot and _____ into the depths of the sea" (Micah 7:19, NIV).

"He saved us, not because of works done by us in righteousness, but according to his own mercy, by the washing of _____ of the Holy Spirit" (Titus 3:5, ESV).

When you find yourself feeling bound by guilt and shame, give it to the Lord in prayer, and speak the Word of God over those opposing thoughts, for that is only an attack of the enemy, wanting you to doubt who you are in Christ and deny the promises of God, stated in His Word.

> Therefore, if anyone is in Christ, the new creation has come: The old has gone, the new is here! All this is from God, who reconciled us to himself through Christ and gave us the ministry of reconciliation: that God was reconciling the world to himself in Christ, not counting people's sins against them. And he has committed to us the message of reconciliation. We are therefore Christ's ambassadors, as though God were making his appeal through us. We implore you on Christ's behalf: Be reconciled to God. God made him who had no sin to be sin for us, so that in him we might become the righteousness of God. (2 Corinthians 5:17–21 NIV)

Toe-to-Toe

In order that Satan might not outwit us. For we are not unaware of his schemes.
—2 Corinthians 2:11 (NIV)

One step at a time. One punch at a time. One round at a time.—Rocky Balboa

A year had passed since the enemy's attempt to attack me and my marriage—a battle in which I got the victory yet again. A girlfriend, who was experiencing what she also recognized as an attack on her marriage, called me to ask that I specifically pray for her during that time.

That particular day, the enemy attempted to knock me down several times. I literally felt like I was laughing in his face, because I noticed his numerous attempts to strike (his tactics are never new) and was able to dodge each of them. Later that evening, I was telling David about my day and how the enemy had attempted to scrap with me. Suddenly, I felt an excruciating pain from my neck downward. David rushed me to the emergency room, but after several medical tests at the hospital and, later, follow-up doctor appointments, there was no medical explanation for the pain I experienced. But I knew exactly what it was. The enemy attempted to attack me spiritually and emotionally that day in several ways without success, so he attacked my physical body.

When I spoke to my girlfriend several days later, she explained that on the same day that I had interceded in prayer on behalf of her marriage, not only did I go to the hospital for a sudden pain, but she and another individual she'd asked to pray for her did as well. Each of us went toe-to-toe with the attack of the enemy that day.

When a boxer is preparing for his next fight, he studies his opponent based on previous battles in order to analyze how the opponent moves. Satan has studied you in an attempt to knock you out. Rather than a simple knock-out in the first round, he'll spar with you to test your strength and to wear you out. However, Satan has no new tactics. You must study your opponent in order to be prepared and alert for his next move—"one step at time, one punch at a time, one round at a time"—and you will have the victory.

Satan and his demons flee at the Word of the God. In the following section, identify various attacks of the enemy and scriptures that you can use to resist each specific opposition toward you.

Attacks of the Enemy	Resist with the Word of God

"Behold, I give you the authority to trample on serpents and scorpions, and over all the power of the enemy, and nothing shall by any means hurt you" (Luke 10:19 NKJV).

The Lord God is the substance of the very things that the enemy attempts to attack—our spiritual, mental, and emotional health. Therefore, He gives us power over the enemy that nothing shall by any means hurt you. When you feel that you are in the boxing ring with the enemy, have peace in knowing that you are not up against the ropes alone. For the Lord our God sends His angels to guard you (reference Psalm 91:11).

I Shall Not Be Moved

Put on the full armor of God [for His precepts are like the splendid armor of a heavily-armed soldier], so that you may be able to [successfully] stand up against all the schemes and the strategies and the deceits of the devil. 12 For our struggle is not against flesh and blood [contending only with physical opponents], but against the rulers, against the powers, against the world forces of this [present] darkness, against the spiritual forces of wickedness in the heavenly (supernatural) places. 13 Therefore, put on the complete armor of God, so that you will be able to [successfully] resist and stand your ground in the evil day [of danger], and having done everything [that the crisis demands], to stand firm [in your place, fully prepared, immovable, victorious]. (Ephesians 6:11–13 AMP)

Two months had passed since the hospital incident and the sudden pains—the toe-to-toe with the enemy. At this point he was tired of losing this battle with me, and one thing was for sure: he does not give up easily.

I was pulling an all-nighter in preparation for our son Jordan's birthday party. Jordan had requested a cake, cupcakes, cake pops, and a variety of doughnuts, all made by Mommy. As promised, what the birthday boy wants, the birthday boy gets. The whole house was asleep—baby Caleb on the couch, Jordan in his bed upstairs, and David in our room. So I decided to call a girlfriend who lives in another time zone; I knew she'd be up and willing to chat.

It was so good to hear her voice. We caught up on the happenings of our day-to-day lives. She was excited to share that it had been two months since her last spell with a medical condition that caused her to become incoherent and experience loss of awareness for a time. During our conversation, the Holy Spirit led me to speak into a situation and call out the spirits that were attempting to impart themselves into her life through another individual. It was in that moment that I heard—as clear as the conversation between my friend and me—*"I hate you!"*

I said to my friend, "Did I offend you?"

"No. Why?" she responded. "Everything you're saying, I needed to hear."

"Did you just say 'I hate you'?"

"No, but I heard something too. I thought it was interference on the phone line."

And then I knew it was time for me to put on my armor and prepare for war! I explained, "Satan does not want us to have this conversation. He wants you to remain just where he has you, and he is angry with me for being obedient to the Holy Spirit. And to think I thought I was calling to have someone to talk to while making these doughnuts!"

By this time it was around three in the morning, just past midnight for her. As we continued to discuss the move of God, I noticed that she hadn't responded to my last comment. I called her name a few times and when she didn't respond, I figured that she must have fallen asleep.

As soon as I hung up the phone, an overwhelming feeling came over me that seemed to fill my house. It was then that I began to pray aloud in the Spirit while using the authority given by God to cast out Satan and his demons, for they were *not* welcome in my home. And what I saw in the Spirit was a host of angels encamped around me; the enemy and his spiritual forces had no power to come against me. I began to pray in each room of the house, casting out the enemy. I went over to the couch, grabbed the baby, and prayed over him. He was still asleep in my arms as we went upstairs. I walked into Jordan's room to pray, and as I was praying, Jordan, in his sleep, was used by the Holy Spirit—he began to pray as well. (How awesome is our God!) I then went into my room to pray over my husband and laid the baby next to him.

When I made my way back downstairs into the kitchen, a tremendous sense of peace filled the air, for in the name of Jesus they had to flee! Not long after, my friend called me back. I said, "Hey, you fell asleep!"

She responded, "No, I think I had one of my spells again."

The devil is a liar!

"Then Jesus said to him, "Be gone, Satan! For it is written, "You shall worship the Lord your God and him only shall you serve. Then the devil left him, and behold, angels came and were ministering to him" (Matthew 4:10–11 ESV).

Satan is not omnipresent like God; he can only be in one place at one time. Therefore, he does not work alone. He employs other demonic beings in multifaceted ways to work and fight against your body, soul, and spirit.

You must be cautious of what you open yourself to and in what you allow yourself to indulge. Even the things that may not appear harmful could become a welcome mat to unwanted spirits. You have the authority to cast out demons and rebuke the enemy. In Jesus's name, stand firm and let the enemy know:

Satan, you *cannot* have my *mind*!

Satan, you *cannot* have my *marriage*!

Satan, you *cannot* have my *children*!

Satan, you *cannot* have my *victory*!

Satan, you *do not* have my *soul*, for I belong to the great I AM!"

Use the following space to journal what you've gained from this week's study. Talk to the Lord in your writing about something that you may need to submit to Him to resist the ploys of the enemy, and use the authority given to you through your anointing to rebuke Satan.

Journal

Journal

Journal

The mountains shake before You
the demons run and flee
at the mention of the name King of Majesty.
There is no power in hell
or any who can stand
before the power and the presence of the Great I am
—*Phillips, Craig & Dean, "Great I Am"*

The Heart of Worship

You search much deeper within
Through the way things appear
You're looking into my heart

I'm coming back to the heart of worship
And it's all about You,
It's all about You, Jesus
I'm sorry, Lord, for the thing I've made it
When it's all about You
—Matt Redman, "The Heart of Worship"

As I sit at my computer, ready to get into today's study—after secluding myself in the best way possible from three little ones, with headphones on to silence the outside noise but close enough to assist David with the kids as needed—I am brought to tears as I listen to and meditate on the above lyrics. This is my worship.

"But the hour is coming, and now is, when the true worshipers will worship the Father in spirit and truth; for the Father is seeking such to worship Him. God is Spirit, and those who worship Him must worship in spirit and truth" (John 4:23–24 NKJV).

In previous weeks we have discussed authenticity and transparency of ourselves, with others, and with God about ourselves. God desires each of us to worship Him and to do so with authenticity.

More than a Song

To worship God is to declare that He is worthy; and we do so with our words, our minds, and our bodies as an expression of our hearts through speaking, listening, and/or doing. The songwriter acknowledges the necessity of worshipping God in truth, with "more than just a song," for what He requires of us is much deeper than just words; rather, it is what is in our hearts.

Your relationship with the Lord is personal, and your worship toward Him should be made personal as well. Whether your worship includes singing a song of praise, dancing, kneeling and bowing in submission, raising your hands, shouting hallelujah, or tears streaming down your face, make it more than the action of what you're doing, and enter into a place of worship *in spirit and in truth*.

I'm Coming Back—It's All about You, Jesus

When you worship the Lord for His glory, His wonder, and the truth in His Word, you may find yourself in repentance and consecration unto Him. That is what the songwriter is describing when he said, "I'm coming back to the heart of worship; I'm sorry Lord for the thing I've made it for it's all about you!"

When we are doing work for the Lord, we can easily become distracted by *what* we're doing and lose sight of *why* we are doing it. We become puffed up with Christian pride. Remind yourself who the center of your worship is, and ask the Holy Spirit to remove all distractions surrounding you.

Read 1 Chronicles 16:23–31.

    1.   How does this scripture describe the Lord?

2. In what ways are you called to worship God, according to this scripture?

3. What are the lyrics to a worship song currently in your heart?

Lord, we come to You in spirit and in truth with a heart of thanksgiving, a mouth full of praise, and a mind focused on You, Father. Lord, Your word says it, and therefore we declare that Your glory is among the nations, for even the heavens praise Your name! Father, we come into Your presence humbled by Your majesty. We worship You in the splendor of Your holiness, for we rejoice in who You are—the King of kings, the Lord of lords, the great I AM. Amen.

The Healing Begins

No matter who you are, despite your walk in life, and regardless of a lack or generous proportion of possessions and accomplishments, you have hurts, disappointments, fears, setbacks, failures, and trials; the list goes on. It's in those times that you desire God the most. You need His guidance, His comfort, His love, His *promise* that everything will be all right. You need healing, but what you really want is for the situation (the hurt, disappointment, fear, setbacks, failure, trial, etc.) is for the experience to have never happened at all, and you ask God, *why?*

"And not only this, but [with joy] let us exult in our sufferings and rejoice in our hardships, knowing that hardship (distress, pressure, trouble) produces patient endurance; and endurance, proven character (spiritual maturity); and proven character, hope and confident assurance [of eternal salvation]" (Romans 5:3–4 AMP).

One morning, while scrolling through the pictures and posts from others on social media, I "liked" someone's shared meme that read:

"I regret opening up to some people, they didn't deserve to know me like that."

Initially, I agreed. I thought back on some personal conversations that I so wished I could take back. But in that moment, the Holy Spirit reminded me that my life is His. Everything I have experienced—the hurts, the disappointments, the fears, the setbacks, the failures, the trials—has been a testament to His ability to work in and through me! And those with whom I have shared things, who may not have been sent to pray with or for me, can witness His glory in yet another person who is not without sin but *simply redeemed*!

Jesus was beaten and battered, pierced for our transgressions and bruised for our iniquities, yet by His wounds we were healed in the process. Your healing occurs in the midst of your sufferings and hardships, not after. Therefore, in the midst of your travails, rejoice, for your healing (your endurance, your spiritual maturity, your character, your hope, and your confident assurance in your Redeemer) has already begun.

Have you ever heard someone ask this question (or maybe you've asked it yourself)—"Why does God allow bad things to happen to good [and/or godly] people?" Many times that question is posed by someone who is hurting. No one can explain why God allows certain things to happen, but we do know is that every time you suffer and survive, you receive a deeper experience with the Spirit of God. You have the ability to help others in their difficult journeys.

Read 1 Peter 4:12–19.

1.   What is to be expected? (1 Peter 4:12)

2.   How should we respond to trials? (1 Peter 4:13–14)

3.   Why should we examine ourselves in trials? (1 Peter 4:15–18)

4.   Who should we commit ourselves to in trials? (1 Peter 4:19)

"So we do not lose heart. Though our outer self is wasting away, our inner self is being renewed day by day. For this light momentary affliction is preparing for us an eternal weight of glory beyond all comparison, as we look not to the things that are seen but to the things that are unseen. For the things that are seen are transient, but the things that are unseen are eternal" (2 Corinthians 4:16–18 ESV).

Our God is greater, our God is stronger, God you are higher than any other.
Our God is Healer, Awesome in Power, Our God! Our God!
And if our God is for us, then who could ever stop us.
And if our God is with us, then what could stand against.
—Chris Tomlin, "Our God"

Moving Mountains

Spirit lead me where my trust is without borders
Let me walk upon the waters
Wherever You would call me
Take me deeper than my feet could ever wander
And my faith will be made stronger
In the presence of my Savior
—Hillsong United, "Oceans"

He answered, "Because of your little faith [your lack of trust and confidence in the power of God]; for I assure you and most solemnly say to you, if you have [living] faith the size of a mustard seed, you will say to this mountain, 'Move from here to there, 'and [if it is God's will] it will move; and nothing will be impossible for you. (Matthew 17:20 AMP)

During a ministry meeting for our intercessory prayer group, we were sharing prayer requests and reports of praise with one another. As I sat there taking heed of what my peers were sharing, I wondered if I should share a request that I had. It was big for me, but was it too small for this group? Just then Mrs. K. shared a praise report.

She explained that her daughter, who had studied to become a lawyer, was discouraged after failing the bar exam. She had only one more opportunity to pass the exam in order to practice law. From the time she received the news that her daughter had to take the exam yet again, Mrs. K. did what many praying mothers would do—she immediately went to the Lord.

After several hours in the car, driving from Washington, DC, to Roanoke, Virginia, where her daughter would take a repeat exam, Mrs. K waited in the car as her daughter made her way into the testing center.

How appropriate that the exam was administered in Roanoke, a city surrounded by mountains. It's located immediately west of the Blue Ridge Mountains and east of the Allegheny Mountains.

Just as her daughter entered into the building, Mrs. K. received an unction to exit her car and she began to walk around the lot to intercede for her daughter, praying that she would pass the exam. In the next moment, the Holy Spirit compelled her to stop where she stood and look up—and what she saw in the Spirit was that the two largest mountains in her direct view were being moved! She knew in that instant that the Lord was answering her prayers, as she was reminded of *mountain-moving faith*.

Her daughter indeed passed the exam, and her testimony of faith encouraged me to share my prayer request, which involved my having to retake the CPCE (Counselor Preparation Comprehensive Examination), after waiting an entire year following graduation, because I was terrified that I would fail as I had the first time. I'd figured that if I didn't share this request, then I wouldn't have to admit that I failed for the second time—if that was to happen. In that moment, though, my faith was made stronger in the presence of my Savior. I knew that I needed to be reminded of my own mountain-moving faith with the story shared by Mrs. K. (In case you're wondering, I passed!)

"And whatever you ask in My name, that I will do, that the Father may be glorified in the Son. If you ask anything in My name, I will do it" (John 14:13–14 NKJV).

Neither Mrs. K.'s daughter nor I passed the exam *simply* for having faith in faith or for having faith in our own desires. Rather, our faith is in God and in His Word. Scripture explains that we go to the Lord and make our requests known to Him in His name, and it will be done for those things *according to His will and purpose*. I know that my career path is according to God's will, as He has allowed my gifts in the natural and spiritual to be aligned. Passing my exam in order to move forward in His purpose was necessary. Therefore, it also was necessary to put my trust in Him.

Read Matthew 17:14–21.

1.   What is your reaction to Jesus's response to the disciples in this passage?

"So I brought him to your disciples and they could not cure him" (Matthew 17:16).

"Why could we not cast it out?" (Matthew 17:19).

"Because of your unbelief; for assuredly I say to you if you have faith as a mustard seed you will say to this mountain 'Move from here to there' and it will move; and nothing will be impossible for you" (Matthew 17:20).

It appears that the disciples may have been ashamed that they were not able to cast out the demon that possessed the child in the passage, as it's stated "the disciples came to Jesus privately" (Matthew 17:19). Jesus's response in verse 20 is not to acclaim "little faith," for it was their little faith that prevented their ability to cast out the demon. His acknowledgement of "having faith as a mustard seed" is not to promote having small faith and remaining there; rather, He demonstrated having faith that starts small and continues to grow.

2. What mountains do you desire to be moved in your life?

3. Write a personal prayer exercising your faith. Watch the mountains be moved as your faith becomes stronger in the Lord.

"Now faith is the substance of things hoped for, the evidence of things not seen" (Hebrews 11:1).

What Would You Ask For?

God appeared to Solomon by dream at night and said, "Ask. What shall I give you?" and Solomon asked for *wisdom* (1 Kings 3).

It was my senior year of undergrad and a lot seemed to be happening that year in every aspect of my life. I went to Washington, DC, to visit one of my closest high school friends (Vic) and his family and to hang out in the city for two days.

It took an entire day for the two of us to catch up; we enjoyed each other's company and shared recent experiences, difficult decisions, God's grace, and laughter. After getting ready for bed, the two of us stayed up until two in the morning—all because of one question. Vic knocked on the guest room door and said, "Jess, can I ask you something? What are you asking God for?"

And my response was, "Wisdom."

That moment turned into a deeper conversation filled with discernment, prayer, and praise as Vic (with eyes full of tears) stated, "Jess, the Lord just told me to tell you that He loves you immensely and that you will receive all that you have asked for." I then began to cry, as I was receptive of what the Spirit was sharing with me through my friend. As with Solomon (1 King 3:10—12), God was pleased with my request.

Spiritual wisdom is having an intimacy with God through the understanding of His Word and His commandments and the ability to apply that toward living holy and righteous in the Lord. *Wisdom* is a translation of the Greek word *sophia*, which means the application of knowledge and understanding. Seeking knowledge and understanding alone is not enough; once it's received we have to apply it to our lives as well.

"The [reverent] fear of the Lord is the beginning (the prerequisite, the absolute essential, the alphabet) of wisdom; A good understanding and a teachable heart are possessed by all those who do the will of the Lord; His praise endures forever" (Psalm 111:10 AMP).

Wisdom begins with our reverent fear and praise for the Lord, a deep acceptance of God's holiness, and the ability to glean understanding from the pages of the Bible. Wisdom can be defined as the ability to recognize right from wrong and holy from unholy. Through the Spirit, those who posses wisdom at times are used to reveal the truth and understanding to others in order to implore the transformation of one's heart.

Read Proverbs 2–4.

What practical insight have you gained from this passage regarding how to pursue wisdom?

The request for God's wisdom is not to be taken lightly. It is a passionate pursuit that requires not only knowledge alone but assistance by the application on your own life and the boldness to be used by God for the transformation of lives around you. Are you willing to commit to wisdom, to understanding, and to the transformation of your own life through intimacy with the Word of God?

If you desire wisdom and are willing to commit to making God's Word a daily part of your life, make that petition here. (I'm doing it with you.)

Signature: _____

Date:_____

Warning: This is a petition between you and God. If you have signed it, be prepared to experience Him in ways you may not have before—through the reading of His Word, during your prayer time, interaction with others, or the reception of a new reflection of self.

"If any of you lacks wisdom, let him ask of God, who gives to all liberally and without reproach, and it will be given to him" (James 1:5 NKJV).

Amen: Last Session

How He set my feet
On solid ground
It makes me want to shout
Hallelujah, Thank you, Jesus
Lord. you're worthy
Of all the glory, and all the honor
And all the praise
—Shane & Shane, "When I Think about the Lord"

"And having been set free from sin, you became slaves of righteousness" (Romans 6:18 NKJV).

The theme of this study is "Simply Redeemed." On day one, it was defined as follows:

> *Simply*—nothing more than: only/merely; without any question
> *Redeemed*—to make something that is [unpleasant] better or acceptable; to buy back [as in stock or bond]

You are no longer controlled by unrighteousness; you are dominated by righteousness.

My prayer for you is that once you reach the last word at the end of these pages, you will continue to seek God, continue to engage with Him daily through genuine talks with Him and a desire for wisdom through His Word, and continue to be humbled by the Holy Spirit so that you may be used daily for the edification and transformation of others.

Use this Bible study as a daily devotional. Go back and study each of the scriptures and teachings that were provided. Reread your responses and answer again, so that you may receive a front-row seat to the transformation that God has fulfilled and continues to fulfill within you.

Throughout this study, how have you experienced transformation? What personal encounters with God have you faced? How was your ego crushed and rebuilt with a spiritual awakening? Who have you become, and where do you desire your continual evolution to take you spiritually and naturally? Answer in detail in the journal pages that follow (reading continues following your journal entry).

Journal

Journal

Journal

Journal

Journal

Journal

Journal

"For we ourselves were also once foolish, disobedient, deceived, serving various lusts and pleasures, living in malice and envy, hateful and hating one another. But when the kindness and the love of God our Savior toward man appeared, not by works of righteousness which we have done, but according to His mercy He saved us, through the washing of regeneration and renewing of the Holy Spirit" (Titus 3:3–5 NKJV).

You are in the hands of your heavenly Father, the King of kings! As His daughter, you are an heir to His throne. You have been paid with the ultimate cost, and you are worthy of love and infinite value, for you, my sister, are simply redeemed.

> I am your sister; can I show you the way?
> We'll walk this road together
> Yes we will, we'll take it day by day
> By faith I know we'll make this journey's end
> Make no mistake about it
> You have been redeemed, redeemed
>
> Jesus, He paid to set you free
> So offer up your life to Him accept His love
>
> Simply redeemed
> —Heather Headley, "Simply Redeemed"

Testimonials

Simply Redeemed has been such a blessing to me. It allowed me to disconnect from this chaotic world and get intimate with God. The Bible studies were right on point; guided by scriptures that are now hidden in my heart. The sisterly gatherings helped me to be more transparent with God but also with others. Simply Redeemed is more than just a movement; it's a life-changing experience.

—Ashley Harris, Virginia

As a woman, as a mother, as someone who wears many hats and has many roles, Simply Redeemed allowed me to take a pause for some quality "me time." It was like having a spa day, where I received pampering for my soul—a transparent and true, honest look at me and things that were buried so deep that they could have [gone] unnoticed. I obtained answers to the hard questions I never asked myself, but needed to. This study was similar to a one-on-one spiritual counseling session between me and God, where I was safe to reveal and release so much of my truth and be renewed.

—Tawana Ross, Maryland

Simply Redeemed is truly a devotional guided by the Holy Spirit. Jessica Jemmott was led by Him *every step* of the way. It changed my life and reignited a flame in my heart. As a result, my relationship with God has grown. I have fallen so much deeper in love with Him than I ever was before. If I had to sum up this book in three words, they would be growth, love, and increase.

—Robin Azemar Brown, Maryland

Simply Redeemed Bible study has helped me to strengthen my faith with the Lord. This experience has changed my life in more ways than I could ever explain. I am finally establishing the long overdue and much needed relationship with Him.

—Arlene Goden, Virginia

Since joining the *Simply Redeemed* Bible study, my outlook on life has changed. I have a better sense of self, and my faith and belief in God continues to grow through prayer and through scripture. Psalm 23.

—Isa Woodberry, Virginia

Simply Redeemed is an answer to prayer! The intimate connection I have to the study is spiritually felt. Every word written on the pages addressed things I had prayed for a year prior to receiving the lessons.

—Chantée Adams, Virginia

Being a part of the *Simply Redeemed* Bible study is beyond amazing. The Lord, through this study, continues to remind me that He too is on life's journey with all of us. This Bible study and devotional has allowed a group of women to fellowship and share and witness to each other how God continues to reveal Himself to us and do phenomenal things in our lives. I cannot think of a more opportune time to cater to your spiritual curiosity and join the movement—for we are all loved and *simply redeemed*.

—Karyn Perkins, Maryland

Transparency is key! Healing is derived from the truth.

—Audry Tonie Jones, Virginia

I am in awe of the focus, discipline, and validation I received from being a part of the *Simply Redeemed* six-week Bible study and instruction. Each week I reflected and experienced growth in my understanding of who God is and His role in my life. It gave me a renewal in my faith and surpassed my expectation. It placed me in a spirit of gratitude because I was able to reflect over how God has been there every step of the way. It was simple yet satisfying. I am forever grateful for Jessica and this experience.

—Georggetta Howie, Washington, DC

The beautiful thing about the Simply Redeemed Bible study is that it is intended to encourage the reader, either reader and book, or in a group setting. Group sessions for Simply Redeemed are designed for groups that meet for one to two hours (depending on how large your group is) to encourage intimate discussion and connection among each other. With the incline of online communication, I had the opportunity to schedule group sessions bi-weekly with active group communication and participation online. The opportunities to lead a group with Simply Redeemed are vast, including small groups, online groups, online live, retreats, conferences, and more! I encourage you to tailor your group time and format to fit the specific needs of your setting, as well as the needs of the participants.

When the Lord told me to "move with urgency" and start this women's Bible study, my thought was, *I've never led a Bible study before.* And then I was reminded of my experiences as a prayer leader in my dorm in college and, most importantly, my experiences in my career as a group counselor. Look how God prepared me in the natural for His purposes in the spiritual!

Prepare

If you feel led to lead a group using *Simply Redeemed*, be encouraged in knowing that you, as an individual, and your ministry among your group have been prayed over. Here are a few key tips as you prepare for your weekly sessions:

o First and foremost, pray for yourself as the leader. Ask the Holy Spirit to guide you, speak through you, and to work through the daily studies to increase personal and spiritual growth and intimacy with the Lord/and authenticity among the participants.

o Secure a location. When securing a location for your group sessions, be intentional about it. Use a location with limited distractions and a comfortable environment that meets the needs of every participant, as well as providing (or discussing) child-care options, if applicable. Plan ahead by ensuring that you coordinate with the location manager (if necessary) and calendar scheduling, and provide refreshments. (After the first session, it may be helpful to enlist volunteers to provide refreshments for the remaining gatherings.)

o Plan ahead by deciding what material you will cover during your sessions. You may use the discussion questions provided or include your own.

o Recommended materials: binder/notebook (for your own personal notes during sessions), prayer journal, name tags, pens, prayer cards, basket, sign-in sheet (retrieve names, e-mail addresses, and Facebook information if you plan to create an online community), refreshments, and Internet access.

Group In-Session

During each group session, use the first twenty minutes for sign-in, social interaction, and refreshments. Encourage participants to write in the prayer journal for anything that they may be praying for or are in need of prayer for at the time. (You will diligently pray over the requests that are documented in your personal time with the Lord.) Follow up during group sessions to identify any answered prayers and praise.

As you engage with your participants between group sessions, encourage everyone to increase time-management skills by completing the daily studies to get the most out of this exciting journey. Be sensitive, however, in your approach by ensuring that you are not causing your participants to feel pressured to complete the assignments or guilty if they do not.

I encourage you, as the leader, to be an active participant in the discussions, but be mindful that you are not taking over the sessions with your personal stories and reflection. You are to encourage active participation from the group members, but I discourage you from publically pointing out individuals who may not be as active as others. If you find that one or two individuals tend to dominate the discussion, be sure that you graciously redirect the group discussion to include others.

One thing that I learned as a counselor within a group environment is that there will be moments where you will experience group silence during reflection—embrace it! Your group members are using those moments to reflect on what someone shared, how it connects with their own stories, and, most important, how the Spirit is moving at that time. As you are aware of the needs of the members, the time allotted, and your group plan, don't rush through the questions to get each one in. Use this time to build personal connections (your online community is a great place to present questions and group discussion that were not posed during the group gathering).

Group termination is always a difficult task. If you are starting a group with *Simply Redeemed*, I encourage you to begin discussing the termination process two weeks prior to the end. If applicable, I encourage you to continue to communicate via online and/or meet with the group that you have started by introducing a new study and/or encouraging one of your members to lead or introduce another study to maintain the connection that has started.

We all love reminders of a great time. This is also an opportunity to present solidarity by encouraging your participants to purchase one of the several apparel options or accessories available online at www.simplyredeemedt335.com or our Etsy Shop SimplyRedeemedT335.

Sample Sessions (based on a bi-weekly schedule)
End of Week 1—Group Session 1

o **Group Icebreaker**: Encourage each participant to "share one thing you like about yourself."

o **Group Reflection**: Review this week's activities.

   o Reflect on the meaning of simply redeemed.

   o What personal applications has God given you this week?

   o What personal need or issue was exposed this week?

   o What encouraged you this week?

   o What convicted you?

   o What "I never thought of that before" insight did you receive?

o **Introduce Prayer Cards**

   o Ask each individual to write one or several current prayers on the back of the prayer cards [provided in book], fold, and place in basket. At the end of each session you will have the participants pull a card out of the basket (not their own), and encourage them to diligently pray daily over those prayers written on the card by their group partners.

o **Wrap Up**

   o Play the song "Simply Redeemed" by Heather Headley. Encourage the group to close their eyes, listen to the lyrics, and reflect.

   o Have everyone pick a prayer card out of the basket (previously filled out by group member).

   o End in prayer and dismiss.

o *Encourage discussion in your online group.*

End of Weeks 2 and 3—Group Session 2

o **Group Icebreaker**: Encourage each participant to "share the best thing that happened this week."

o **Group Reflection**: Review weeks 2 and 3

   o What are your favorite promises from God?

o "Behind the Curtain"—Romans 8:38–39. Nothing can separate me from the love of God! Reflect.

o "Seeking God"/"You just watched"—reflect on difficult lessons or consequences.

o "Perfect Fit"/spiritual growth—where/how have you grown?

o "Love Letter"—were you able to meet the goal of loving yourself?

o What "I never thought of that before" insight did you receive?

o What lesson(s) were most difficult? Why?

o What did the Holy Spirit expose that you attempted not to face?

o What encouraged you?

o What did you learn?

o **Prayer Cards**

o Ask each individual to write one or several current prayers on the back of the prayer cards [provided in book], fold, and place in basket. At the end of each session, you will have the participants pull a card out of the basket (not their own) and encourage them to diligently pray daily over those prayers written on the card by their group partners.

o **Wrap Up**

o Have everyone pick a prayer card out of the basket (previously filled out by group member).

o End in prayer and dismiss.

o *Encourage discussion in your online group.*

End of Week 4—Group Session 3

o **Materials**: Each participant's name in a basket, foot-washing basin (get creative!), towels (one for each participant), pitcher of warm water with soap and essential oils and/or baby oil. (Allow each participant to pick a name out of the basket before beginning the session. Do not discuss today's activity with the members prior to the time you are ready to begin the feet-washing activity. Each foot-washing engagement should be two different people.

o **Group Reflection**: Love/forgiveness/pride—these are all things we experience. Use this time to reflect on how your group was affected by this week's lessons.

o **Feet-Washing Activity:** Week 4 is about love, forgiveness, and humility. This group session encourages the true experience of humility and knocking down the wall of pride through the washing of each other's feet, as Jesus did for His disciples in John 13:1–17.

o Play the song "Simply Redeemed" by Heather Headley. Encourage the group to close their eyes, listen to the lyrics, and reflect.

o Have everyone pick a prayer card out of the basket (previously filled out by group member)/

o End in prayer and dismiss.

o **Prayer Cards/Wrap Up**

o Ask each individual to write one or several current prayers on the back of the prayer cards [provided in book], fold, and place in basket. At the end of each session. you will have the participants pull a card out of the basket (not their own) and encourage them to diligently pray daily over those prayers written on the card by their group partners.

o Begin to introduce group termination plan and process. Order Simply Redeemed apparel online at www.simplyredeemedt335.com, or Etsy Shop—SimplyRedeemedT335.

o End in prayer and dismiss.

o *Encourage discussion in your online group.*

End of Weeks 5 and 6—Final Session

o This final session is a celebration—treat it as such! Use your creativity to plan group session 4. Make a playlist of songs quoted throughout the Bible study.

- o **Group Icebreaker**: _____
- o **Group Reflection**: Review weeks 5 and 6.
    - o
    - o
    - o
    - o

- o **Prayer Journal**
    - o Discuss ongoing prayers and praise reports.

- o **Wrap Up**
    - o
    - o
    - o Discuss plans for the next study or leader (if applicable).
    - o End in prayer and dismiss.

- o *Continue ongoing dialogue and communication in your online group.*

Simply
Redeemed
TITUS 3:3-5

Simply
Redeemed
TITUS 3:3-5

Simply
Redeemed
TITUS 3:3-5

Simply
Redeemed
TITUS 3:3-5

Bibliography

Barnard, Shane, and Everett, Shane. "When I Think About The Lord." on *Carry Away*. Nashville, TN: Inpop Records, 1993.

Dictionary.com, s.v. "pride," accessed March 3, 2016, http://www.dictionary.com/browse/pride

Franklin, Kirk. "Let Me Touch You." on *Whatcha Lookin' 4*. US: GospoCentric Records, 1996.

Greene, Travis. "The HIll". on *The Hill*. US: RCA Inspiration, 2015.

Headley, Heather. "Simply Redeemed." on *Audience of One*. US: K. Thomas, 2009.

Hillsong United. "Oceans (where feet May Fail)." on *Zion (Deluxe Edition)*. Sydney, Australia : J. H. Michael Guy Chislett, 2013.

Jordan, Derrick D. Interview by author. Trussville, AL, December 21, 2015.

Phillips, Randy, Shawn Craig, and Dan Dean. "Great I Am." on *Breathe In*. Fair Tade Services, 2012.

Tomlin, Chris. "Our God." on *And If Our God Is for Us …* US: D. M. Ec Cash, 2010.

Mcfadden, Dave. "Diotrephes & Demetrius - A Cantankerous & A Consistent Christian." *SermonCentral,* accessed March 3, 2016, www.sermoncentral.com/sermons/8220diotrephes--demetrius-8211-a-cantankerous--a-consistent-christian8211-dave-mcfadden-sermon-on-church-discipline-165659.asp

Merriam-Webster.com, s.v. "redeemed," accessed January 31, 2016, http://www.learnersdictionary.com/definition/redeemed

Merriam-Webster.com, s.v. "simply," accessed January 31, 2016, http://www.learnersdictionary.com/definition/simply

Redman, Matt. "The Heart of Worship." on *Intimacy. US: Star Song, 1998.*

About the Author

Jessica Jemmott is an alumna of Liberty University. She has received both a BS in psychology and sociology and an MA in professional counseling, and her desire is to promote psychological, physical, and spiritual health and awareness amongst adolescents, women, and men.

Fifteen years ago, Jessica received a vision from the Lord to create a multifaceted counseling center/café named The Lamp (a.k.a. The Chocolate Lamp) to create an atmosphere for the community that provides services for the needs and desires of all who enter through the doors, a space for refuge from crisis and the happenings of daily life. It is a community counseling center/café that provides expressive art therapies while meeting needs holistically—body, mind, and spirit. It promotes a healthy and safe environment for the self and the community while encouraging unity among cultural divides.

As she works to bring that vision to life, she is currently being prepared for the ministry facet through Simply Redeemed.

Whether through counseling, cooking/baking, expressive arts, sharing thoughts and experiences through written form, and/or ministry, everything that the Lord equips Jessica with to engage with others starts and ends with love—through the expression of the love of Christ.

"Wife, mother (of three), worshiper, entrepreneur, teacher, counselor, sister, friend, daughter, lover, fighter, visionary, prayer warrior, author, woman—whatever the title on whatever day, I am totally loving the woman that I am! As I stand under the covering of the Lord and alongside my husband, I am gaining confidence in the full acceptance of me! I'm no longer the people pleaser I once was, no longer seeking acceptance of others, no longer in bondage of the perceptions of others. My identity is in him who has created me as I am, his prized possession."

#iamredeemed

Printed in the United States
By Bookmasters